D0810343

My Father's People

My Father's People

LOUIS D. RUBIN, JR.

A Family of Southern Jews

Louisiana State University Press
Baton Rouge

Copyright © 2002 by Louis D. Rubin, Jr.
Manufactured in the United States of America
First printing
11   10   09   08   07   06   05   04   03   02
5   4   3   2   1

Designer: Laura Roubique Gleason
Typeface: Minion
Printer and binder: Thomson-Shore, Inc.

Library of Congress Cataloging-in-Publication Data:

Rubin, Louis Decimus, 1923–
   My father's people : a family of Southern Jews / Louis D. Rubin Jr.
     p. cm.
   ISBN 0-8071-2808-2 (cloth : alk. paper)
   1. Rubin family. 2. Jews—South Carolina—Charleston—Biography.
3. Charleston (S.C.)—Biography. I. Title.
   F279.C49 J5787 2002
   975.7'91004924'00922—dc21

2002000454

The paper in this book meets the guidelines for permanence and
durability of the Committee on Production Guidelines for Book
Longevity of the Council on Library Resources. ⊖

For Lee Smith

And Hal Crowther

"Damn them, they are my people. I am one of them, thank God."
—William Watts Ball, *The State That Forgot*

"Riddle me this, and guess him if you can."
—Juvenal, *Satires*, trans. John Dryden

Contents

Illustrations

Acknowledgments

For information from the files of the Hebrew Orphans' Home of Atlanta, I am grateful to Sandra K. Berman, archivist of the William Breman Jewish Heritage Museum, Atlanta.

Mr. Sol Breibart, of Charleston, South Carolina, longtime scholar of the history of the Jews of Charleston, was kind enough to provide me with information from the records of congregation K. K. Beth Elohim.

My brother and sister, Edwin Manning Rubin of New York City and Joan Rubin Schoenes of Richmond, Virginia, provided help and encouragement in the writing of this book. Needless to say, the views and interpretations expressed herein are not necessarily theirs.

My long-ago student, more recently my partner in our publishing venture, Shannon Ravenel Purves, gave this manuscript a close, skillful, imaginative reading.

The chapter entitled "Riddle Me This" appeared in *Southern Review* for fall 2002, and I am grateful to Dave Smith, the editor, for permission to use it here.

L. D. R.
Chapel Hill, North Carolina
August 23, 2001

My Father's People

Prologue

ONE HUNDRED YEARS ago, on a September day in 1902, three little boys were placed aboard a train in Charleston, South Carolina, and sent off to the Hebrew Orphans' Home in Atlanta, Georgia. They were not orphans; both their parents were living. Their father, however, was ill and unable to work, and their mother, with four other children including an infant daughter, was without any source of income.

The youngest of the three boys being sent away was seven years old. The other two were ten and eight. The seven- and eight-year-olds stayed at the Orphans' Home for three years, the ten-year-old for two, before being allowed to return home. Thereafter all three lived reasonably long lives, and as adults none would ever again be in need, nor would their brothers and sisters. Yet the experience of those years remained decisive to their lives and their careers. Much of what they were, and also what they were not, may be in important ways attributed to it.

The seven-year-old was my father, the eight- and ten-year-olds my uncles Manning and Dan. This is a book about them and their family—the father and mother, such as is known about them, and the seven children. I shall try to tell about these people as best I can, while conscious that much will have to be conjecture and that the years that now intervene between them and myself must inevitably distort the perspective, as if they were being seen through a telescope across the haze of a lengthening distance.

A goodly portion of what follows centers on the city of Charleston, where the seven children grew up and where most of them made their homes. It was also where I was raised, though our branch of the family moved away to Richmond, Virginia, in 1942, and only my sister ever returned to Charleston to live as an adult. Even so, I have never thought of any other place as our family's home, and over the course of what are now six full decades since leaving, I doubt that very many years have gone by without my visiting there at least once.

In the fall of 2000, following our last remaining aunt's death that June at age ninety-eight, my sister moved back to Richmond to be with her own children and grandchildren, so that for the first time in some 115 years there are no members of my father's family living in Charleston. It seems unlikely that any will ever move to the city. When I visit Charleston nowadays, it is much like walking onto the stage of a theater where the set with all the flats and properties is in place but the actors and actresses are missing.

I drive along Beaufain Street, by the Colonial Lake. My Aunt Dora will not emerge from the front entrance of the Berkeley Court Apartments and hurry down the walkway to where the Belt Line trolley is waiting for her, the motorman knowing that she will typically be a minute or two late en route to her job on Broad Street.

Two blocks farther west, across Gadsden Street, the tidal flat that was once there has been filled in, and houses are in place all the way to Lockwood Drive along the river. Somewhere in the soil beneath them must be the bones of the old ferryboat *Sappho,* whose decaying wooden hulk once served as a haven for sailboats and rowboats. Not again will my Uncle Manning be found seated on a stone slab along the embankment on a bright Sunday morning, reading the *Romances of Herman Melville.*

This book is not a eulogy, but an effort to know. I wrote it because I wanted to try to understand who my father's family were, and what they meant for and about me. The portraits that follow are subjective, sometimes critical, and always quite personal. Others who knew the family will not agree with all of my conclusions. But I do know this:

whatever may be said of their virtues, there is not a fault or a blemish chronicled here that I do not recognize in myself.

Nostalgia is an impoverishing emotion; it robs our memory of all its complexity. I hope I have avoided it. There were no Good Old Days; my father's generation knew that very well. Yet we *are* our memory, and we exist in Time. What we can know is the distance we have traveled, and where we have been.

The period of human time covered in this book is approximately a century and a decade, beginning in the mid-1880s when my grandparents came to Charleston and ending with the death of the last of their seven children in the year 2000. I have presented the lives and careers of my father and his brothers and sisters in a series of sketches. This has made necessary a certain amount of repetition, but it seemed the only way to get at them, for they were very much distinct individuals. As for their descendants, my own generation and those that follow it, other than as they impacted upon the lives of the generation born in the late nineteenth and early twentieth century they are not part of this story.

This is a Southern story. What happens, with slight modifications, might well have taken place elsewhere in the United States of America. But as it was, these people were part of the South, and their response to their experience was very much in terms of the Southern community. In order to understand this it will not do to say, as Quentin Compson tells his Canadian roommate in William Faulkner's *Absalom, Absalom!*, that "you would have to be born there," because what is striking is the swiftness with which the process that sociologists call "acculturation" took place. For reasons having to do with background and temperament, my father and his family seem to have responded to the life of the Southern community with more than ordinary avidity, perhaps because the historical circumstance of the South during the years when they were growing up was more than ordinarily congenial.

It may be that their own expectations and assumptions were such that, cut off from what for their forebears had been a powerful historical and self-sufficient community tradition, in effect they replaced it with the intense heritage of their new home—which was also a minority enclave within a larger cultural and political entity.

This is a book about them, not myself. I am fortunate to have been one of them.

1

A Family

THE MALES DEPARTED in the order of their arrival. Harry, the patriarch, went first, then Dan, Manning, and last my father, Louis. All the sisters outlived them. Dora, oldest of all her generation, died in her mid-nineties, followed by Essie—Esther—and Ruthie, the youngest and also the longest-lived, who when she died in the year 2000 was ninety-eight years old.

Dora had assumed that, being the firstborn, she would be first to go. "When I'm being buried," she told Manning once, "I don't want you and Harry to laugh."

"You do your part, Dora," Manning replied, "and we'll do ours."

The family had a penchant for macabre humor, my father in particular. He liked to listen to music on the phonograph while at dinner, and once he bought a record of Chopin's Funeral March, on a special version designed for use by funeral parlors. When Dora next visited he placed the record, together with others, on the turntable drop mechanism, and midway in the meal the Funeral March began, with the sepulchral theme sounding again and again, until Dora at length realized what it was she was hearing.

As for what might account for this taste in humor, it may have been the early presence in their lives of so much poverty, death, and illness. In the 1900s both the father and mother were ill, and the family income, never more than barely adequate, fell disastrously—so much so that the three youngest boys were sent to the Hebrew Orphans' Home in Atlanta for several years until their father could work again. The father died in 1911, the mother two years later, both at age fifty.

Neither my father nor my three uncles attended school past the seventh grade; after that they looked for jobs. The same was true for Dora. The two younger girls graduated from high school. Two of the brothers married, two did not. Of the three sisters only Essie married, and not well. Thus, two bachelors and two spinsters out of seven siblings, and of those who married, only four children, three of them my father's. In all, a blighted family—which, however, survived.

For all the early deprivation, in none of them was the acquisitive instinct very strong. Even my father, who was off to a thriving business career until stricken by illness in his mid-thirties, cared more for the show than the profits, as his later years demonstrated. Of the four males, he was least intellectual in bent. The other three were readers, and two became writers. All were, incipiently, highly creative. Under different circumstances, with college educations and without the spectre of childhood insecurity to inhibit their willingness to take chances, what they might have done may scarcely be guessed. They were remarkable men. As for their three sisters, not only the family situation but the time, the place, and the cultural and social expectations served severely to limit them. Dora possessed imagination and a keen sense of humor; these, however, remained unapplied. Of the younger two, there was still less that was striking in their lives.

As best I can, I want to tell about them all—my father, his brothers, and, insofar as there is much to be told, his sisters. Individually and as a family the Rubins were distinct, uncommon entities, conforming to no stereotype I have ever encountered. This was in contrast to the Weinsteins, my mother's family of "normal" second- and third-generation Jews, the merchants and professional men and housewives, all of whom married, had children, grandchildren, lived reasonably contented lives. None had intellectual interests or artistic inclinations; there was not an iconoclast, or an agnostic, among them. They were good people, devoid of mystery. They differed from my father's family as an expanse of field at harvest time might differ from a moonlight landscape by El Greco. I feel no urge to seek to explain them. But as for my father and my uncles, the puzzle remains. What made them into what they were? What impulses drove them? Who were they? Riddle me this.

As is true of so many nineteenth-century immigrant families, almost nothing was handed down about their antecedents beyond the ocean. The father, my grandfather Hyman Levy Rubin, was born in or near Georgenburg, or Eorborg, in what was then East Prussia, about 1862. (My wife, whose people were Protestants of New England origin, had a grandfather named Heman Redfield, and when our own first son was due to arrive she proposed that his name be Heman Hyman Rubin; we settled for Robert.) Hyman's father, Herschel, was a native of Krakovena, a town near Kovno, in present-day Lithuania, and moved to Georgenburg, where his wife's family lived. All these were Russian Jews.

What is known of Herschel does not come from his son, who like most Jewish immigrants from eastern Europe would appear to have said little or nothing about his family, probably because they wished to start with as little handicap as possible in a new land. It was my Aunt Dora who, through a family named Levin, also living in coastal South Carolina, discovered that Herschel was a learned man, a religious teacher, probably but not certainly a rabbi, who came from a "fine family." In the context of the time and place this would have meant not wealthy or aristocratic but from a rabbinical tradition, versed in Hebrew law and lore. Beyond that, no information about Herschel and his antecedents is available, and given the fate of the Jewish community in that region of virulent anti-Semitism, if there were family or records remaining they doubtless vanished in the fury of the Holocaust.

Hyman Rubin, after his arrival in the United States, married Frances Sanders, whose parents, Robert and Amelia Todman Sanders, had been born in Germany and left for New York from Coblenz on the Rhine River (which seems odd) aboard a sailing ship the day after they were married, not long before the Civil War. My grandfather had a sister who lived in New Jersey, and a nephew who graduated from

Columbia University sometime in the 1890s. My grandmother had Todman relatives who settled in Elmira, New York, and two sisters. One of them, Esther Sanders, was a longtime teacher in the New York City public schools. The other, Rose, married Julius Hoffman, a tailor who served in Company A, First South Carolina Volunteers, during the Civil War and was wounded in action. One family story was that he was shot in the lungs. Another is that the dust from the 1886 Charleston Earthquake ruined his lungs. Since he died in 1897, whatever did him in was seemingly in no great hurry.

Julius Hoffman was originally from Sumter, South Carolina, and moved to Charleston after the Civil War. What seems likely is that Hyman and Fannie Rubin moved from New York City to Charleston because my grandmother's sister Rose had married Julius and was living there. My aunt Dora, who enjoyed being teased about her age, used to say in later years that as proof of her youthfulness she had always claimed that "Mama and Papa hadn't even met at the time of the earthquake," but "that's not as impressive as it once was." The Charleston Earthquake, which was of 7.6 magnitude and killed sixty people, took place on August 31, 1886, and Dora was born January 1, 1888, so Hyman Levy and Fannie Sanders Rubin were married in late 1886 or early 1887.

The Charleston that my Rubin grandparents came down from New York City to live in, probably in 1886, was still in the process of a languishing and very gradual recovery from the defeat of the Civil War, and would indeed remain so for decades to come. The war and the collapse of the Confederacy had stripped it of most of its wealth, greatly diminished its role as exporter of cotton from the Sea Islands and the interior, killed and maimed no small number of its brightest and bravest young men, freed the slaves upon whose labor the economy of the plantations throughout the adjacent Lowcountry depended, left the heart of the city in ruins from fire and bombardment, and administered a devastating shock to the psyche of a community whose ferocious self-esteem had culminated in secession from the Union and the firing on Fort Sumter. Not until the 1880s did the port begin to make a partial recovery. Trade increased to some degree, and a newly developed phosphate industry north of town brought in much-needed money. Still, not until the 1940s and thereafter might the city be said to have fully regained its onetime place in the sun.

As Southern communities went, Charleston was highly cosmopolitan in makeup. To the Anglo-American and Huguenot stock had been added a substantial German and Irish population, and there were numerous Italian, Polish, and Jewish families. After the Civil War thousands of newly freed slaves from the Sea Islands thronged into the city, and more than half its population was African American.

Socially Charleston was intricately layered. The old planter families, mainly Episcopalian and Presbyterian, whose domain lay south of Broad Street, were at the top, and thereafter came Methodists, Lutherans, Baptists, Roman Catholics, Jews, and various denominations of blacks. As often happens in communities with marked social grada tions, the ordering replicated itself among the various ethnic groups. Thus the old Roman Catholic families of French ancestry considered themselves superior to the Catholic newcomers from Ireland and Germany, who in turn looked down on the Italians. The African Americans were arrayed in a hierarchy that ranged from the light-skinned antebellum free men of color—many of whom were artisans, barbers, and merchants—and their families downward to the vast majority of blacks, who had been plantation laborers in slavery days.

As for the Jews, these too were located up and down a social scale. The old, mostly Sephardic families who had been part of the Charleston scene since the late seventeenth and early eighteenth centuries were soon followed by Jews from England and Holland; there was intermarriage with the gentile population, and many ceased to practice Judaism. When the German Jews arrived in numbers in the 1840s and thereafter, they fanned out through the interior and established themselves as merchants. In the 1870s and 1880s there began an influx from central and eastern Europe, which would continue and intensify in the next century when Tsarist pogroms sent millions of Jews fleeing from Russia.

The Reform Jewish movement, begun in Germany, had its American origin in Charleston, although it was to receive its impetus elsewhere. During the 1830s, 1840s, and 1850s the members of congregation K. K. Beth Elohim, which had been founded in 1749, began conducting services in English, did away with the cantor and introduced the choir and organ, dropped the elaborate dietary laws and various purification customs, and otherwise liberalized the methods of worship and observance along lines similar to the Protestant churches.

By no means did all Charleston Jews go along with the change. The division within the congregation during the 1830s resulted in violent disputes, which even came to fisticuffs at meetings in the temple, and much litigation. During the 1850s and 1860s a rival Orthodox congregation was established. Supposedly the issues under dispute were theological; in actuality the schism had social underpinnings. What was involved was participation and status in the Charleston secular community. As each immigrant group went about being assimilated, its members looked down snobbishly on those who followed, as constituting their social inferiors. Obviously the presence of the newcomers reminded them of the differences between themselves and the larger, mainly gentile community, at a time when they were energetically engaged in minimizing those differences. (The same process was taking place throughout the United States and western Europe.)

As might be expected, from the post–Civil War period onward, most of the Jewish immigrants arriving in the United States from central and eastern Europe were traditionally Orthodox in affiliation and belief, and in Charleston as elsewhere these soon grew to outnumber the city's Reform congregation. With certain exceptions, whether a family was Reform or Orthodox—there was no Conservative congregation in Charleston until the 1950s—became a yardstick of assimilation and therefore of social status.

My own family's position in this is somewhat confused. Hyman, raised in the eastern Baltic area, would almost certainly not have been reared as a Reform Jew. Very likely the affiliation was that of Fannie's family, being German Jews in New York City. In Charleston, Hyman and Fannie's children grew up in the Reform Jewish congregation, K. K. Beth Elohim. It was also Fannie's sister Rose's affiliation and that of her husband, Julius Hoffman. When Julius died in 1897 he was buried in an older Jewish cemetery, and upon Rose's death in the 1920s she was interred at his side.

In any event, it would be difficult to explain just what any such assumption of status could based upon, since neither relative wealth—quite the contrary—nor relative length of American residence, in my grandfather's instance at least, could account for it. Yet my own Reform generation was schooled to look down upon more recent, less Americanized arrivals, and the attitude did not really change until after the Second World War.

From what I have been able to gather, my grandfather was not a notably religious person, for all that his father and his forebears in Europe were probably rabbis and religious teachers. Why it was that he came south is unknown. Whatever the reason may have been, the streets of the late nineteenth and turn-of-the-century South did not exactly turn out to be paved with gold for Hyman Rubin and his family. Nor did the energy and enterprise that characterized the lives of his sons manifest themselves in his response to the time and place.

My Aunt Dora always said that Hyman should have been a scholar. Clearly he was not fitted to be a businessman. He was much too trusting, Dora said, allowing customers to run up large bills that remained unpaid. At one point during the 1890s he was operating a grocery store in the town of Summerville, twenty-five miles from Charleston. My Uncle Harry told me that it was proposed to his father that he sell liquor, which although a violation of state law would have been winked at by the local authorities; if he did he could expect a great deal of business. His response was that he would rather starve before doing so, and, my uncle added, "we darn well nearly did!" (My guess is that this occurred during the "Dispensary War" between Governor, later Senator,

"Pitchfork Ben" Tillman and the older Establishment, in which the Up-country politico's efforts to regulate the sale of alcoholic beverages was heavily opposed by the Lowcountry leadership, including the liquor interests.)

It was in 1902 that my grandfather was invalided by heart attacks. Within a period of less than fourteen years my grandmother had given birth to eight children, seven of whom survived, and she was unable to care for them all, nor was there any money coming in. The three younger boys in the family were sent to the Orphans' Home in Atlanta. Later Hyman recovered sufficiently to operate a small store near the railroad station in Florence, South Carolina. The mother and family stayed on in Charleston, where my father, two of his brothers, and my Aunt Dora had jobs, while one brother, Dan, was a newspaper reporter in Birmingham, Alabama.

When my father died in 1970 the following letter was found among his papers:

H. RUBIN

——— Dealer in ———

General Merchandise

GENTS FURNISHING   GOODS AND NOTIONS

Florence, S.C., August __4__ , 19_11_

Dear Lewis [sic]

Your letter reciv'd Am glad you ar well I forgot To write To Mama She must Send Back the chicken coop as that dont belong to me to Send by Exp J. J. Avant Exp Agent Will might have efue [a few] *more chickens next month to Sheep* [ship] *have nothing else To write So will close with love my Boy your loving Father*

HLR

If anyone has any doubts about America being the Promised Land for the Jews of central and eastern Europe, let it be noted that of the four sons of the author of that letter, one became a newspaper editor, one a playwright with five Broadway plays to his credit, and one wrote and took the color photographs for a book that has been in print for several decades.

A quiet man, Hyman Levy Rubin died in Florence, a hundred miles from his family, at age fifty, approximately five months after he wrote that letter. He liked classical music, and his favorite book, which according to my Aunt Dora he read and reread, was a sentimental English novel, *Ships That Pass in the Night*, by Beatrice Harraden. He also liked Dickens's *The Old Curiosity Shop*. My Uncle Harry, then twenty-two years old, traveled to Florence to close out his store. A judge in Florence, in a letter to the family about Hyman, paraphrased the Apostle Paul; my grandfather, he said, was "an Israelite in whom there was no guile"—a kind of oblique compliment, to be sure, though surely not intended that way.

I have a snapshot of my father and my grandfather seated together on a bench in Charleston, I think in White Point Gardens. To judge from my father's appearance he was fourteen or fifteen years old, which would place the occasion about 1910. In 1910 my grandfather was still in his late forties, but his hair is almost snow-white. His full moustache is dark. Both are dressed in coat and tie, left legs crossed over right, and flat-brimmed straw boaters in their left hands. In his right hand my grandfather is holding the handle of an umbrella. On the lapel of my father's coat is a round decoration of some kind, too large for normal wear as a lapel pin, which leads me to think that the occasion for the photograph might have been that of his confirmation from K. K. Beth Elohim; if so I possess the gold pin, engraved *First Honor — Louis D. Rubin — 1910.*

The family resemblance is striking: high forehead, angular face, prominent nose, deep-set eyes with thick brows, somewhat receding chin. My three uncles possessed the same physiognomy, as did two of my aunts; it is also my brother's, and was my first cousin's. If my own second son, Bill, could have been photographed seated on the bench along with his grandfather and great-grandfather, he would have been more than a foot taller, but in facial appearance they would have seemed almost identical.

In a novel I once tried to characterize my uncles and aunts, seated together on our front porch: "They were a family, all right, but a family made up of very private people, who seemed to look out at the world from a vast interior distance." The eyes, not exactly mournful so much as reclusive, were the dominant feature; all members of the family, of whatever generation, possess them, as if they constituted a genetic talisman of some kind.

Once I was looking through a book about the history of firearms, and I came upon a photograph of a nineteenth-century Swiss inventor. There was something about it that caused me to look more closely. The visage of a uniformed man was staring out at me, sad-faced, moustached, with the identical deep-set, pensive eyes. Underneath was the caption: "Major Schmidt-Rubin."

It is my hunch that there are only a limited supply of basic, inherited physiognomies, and that rather than being blended with others these are passed on pretty much intact from generation to generation. If it were possible to view movie footage taken a hundred years ago showing the inhabitants of the Jewish district of the town in East Prussia where my grandfather's people lived, I might very well be able to identify by sight my own kin walking around. But there would be none of their descendants present there today.

My Uncle Dan, the only one who would talk reflectively and analytically about the family, once observed that his mother and father were not really compatible temperamentally. The father was private, reserved, constrained; the mother was outgoing, affectionate, and demonstrative. Their quarter-century of married life could scarcely have been an idyll. At the time of Hyman Rubin's death, Dan was working as a reporter in Birmingham, and when he traveled home to Charleston for the burial, it was arranged for the train to make an unscheduled stop at Magnolia Crossing, at the northern city limits, where the funeral cortege waited for his arrival before continuing to the cemetery. That was in December of 1911. Fannie Sanders Rubin died

November 29, 1913, of a brain tumor. Not for forty-four years was there another death in the family.

With Dan, Harry, Manning, my father, and Dora earning incomes, the financial burden eased. Esther and Ruthie graduated from Memminger Normal School; Essie became the homemaker, Ruthie found work as a typist. In the early 1920s following World War I and after Harry married and moved to Savannah, the others built a house on Allen Park in Hampton Park Terrace. When my father married, his bride, my mother, came to live with them.

In retrospect, what seems notable, as remarked earlier, is the swiftness, and the thoroughness, of their assimilation into secular American society. There would, of course, have been considerable incentive, economic and social, for it, and particularly in a small Southern city such as Charleston, where not only was the Reform Jewish community a tiny segment of the population, but—and persons living outside the South often do not realize this—there was a tradition from earliest days onward of Jews taking part in the life of the larger secular community. Still, as I have said, there must have been more to it than even that— something in the background, in the way that the members of the family looked at themselves and their identity, that shaped their attitude both toward the everyday life around them and toward their inherited Jewish customs and beliefs. What that was I am by no means sure—I am writing this book in part to try to understand it—but it seems to me to have to do with where their father came from and what his own expectations, however they remained unrealized, may have been. Of that, however, more later.

As I write this, in the first year of a new century, at seventy-seven I am older than any previous male Rubin has lived to be, though the women all lived into their nineties. Several years before her death in 1982 at age ninety-four, Dora, looking at a snapshot of herself and her brothers and sisters taken in the early 1910s, remarked that "when I look at that picture I feel blue." By the 1980s only the three sisters were left. Now all are gone. Such is the nature of life in time. My own feeling, thinking about them, is one of mingled regret and vexation. Regret because a remarkable group of people have vanished. Vexation because during the years when they might have told me so much more than is known about their early years, parents, their antecedents, I did not have foresight enough to ask them.

I suppose it usually happens that way. Not until the young realize that neither they nor those most important to them are immortal, but are instead creatures of time and change, do they begin to look for whatever can be written down. In point of fact I did ask, but with insufficient persistence. Those who if pressed might have told me more were questioned only casually. By the time I began going at it with conscious intention, those family members who might have gone beyond random recollection were all gone. Even my father, who lived so intensely in the present and did not often speculate about the past or view his life within a family context, could have been made to articulate more about where he and his brothers and sisters came from and what they did than has survived.

My aunts, in particular the youngest, were incapable of detailed, exploratory recall. They thought in terms of agreed-upon generalizations. The youngest, Ruthie, who died last of all, insisted that she was too young to remember anything that happened during her childhood—she was twelve when her mother died in 1913—and was adamant in declining to try to reopen what for her was a decisively closed door.

I do not recall them, any of them, engaging in random reminiscence. They did not ever sit around, in my presence at least, and exchange memories of the days when their parents were alive, or when they lived together downtown on Pitt Street or in Allen Park. As a group, except perhaps for Dora, they kept their emotions to themselves. What happened to them and to their parents must have been so distressing, so painful to remember, perhaps so deeply humiliating, that doubtless there was little incentive on their part to relive the memories of that time.

If so it would be understandable. As people grow old they tend to draw satisfaction from being reminded of the particularities of their youthful years, perhaps because the accelerating swiftness of age makes the past seem less and less accessible. But what if one recollects one's earlier life as a struggle to extricate oneself from a desperate situation, and what if remembered details evoke the emotions that accompanied them?

My Uncle Dan, the playwright, was the only one who in conversation with me ever voluntarily brought up any memories that were troublesome or embarrassing. He liked to talk. At the same time he was a very private person, who lived by himself, far away from the family, returning only for periodic visits. I never had the feeling, when I was with him, of casual conversation. It was as if he were thinking out every comment, every response in advance. I am sure that the others must have looked back, and not always with serenity, at their earlier doings, but if so they kept their thoughts to themselves—and very likely they had trained themselves not to allow the past to display itself for conscious inspection for very long. What it comes down to is that by and large they did not *want* to remember.

Even so, I should have insisted. For they were a brave band, and what they did with their lives deserves to be recorded.

2

Dora

DURING THE LATE 1930S, there was a comic strip in the afternoon newspaper entitled "Little Miss Muffet." In one sequence Miss Muffet was being menaced by a scheming schoolmistress, and as the little girl's peril increased, my Aunt Dora grew so alarmed that she arranged to have a neighbor in the Berkeley Court Apartments cut out the Miss Muffet strips from the paper each evening and keep them until her safety had been assured, after which Dora could read them through.

Her way of coping with the parents' illness and their extreme poverty during the late 1890s and early 1900s must have been to try not to think about what was happening. Each of the brothers and sisters responded to that ordeal differently; Dora denied its implications. By remaining resolutely untroubled and declining to allow the deprivation and humiliation to dominate her thoughts, she was able to insulate her consciousness from the full awareness of what was taking place, which otherwise would have been too painful for her to endure. Thereafter it became a lifetime practice. She lived, indeed, in a little world into which brightness, good feelings, honor, and altruism were the only relationships permitted to enter. She used to say of herself that "the Lord will provide," and generally He did.

She was the oldest child, born on New Year's Day, 1888, and as such underwent the full impact of the family's distress. As soon as she could she learned shorthand at a local business college and found work as a stenographer. To bring in extra money in those years of dire poverty, she worked as a hairdresser, going to people's homes and doing her work.

She was a friendly, sociable person, warmhearted and affectionate. She harbored no resentments, was on the best of terms with everyone. For many years she worked as a legal secretary on Broad Street, the city's legal and financial district, where the salaries paid to clerical employees were notoriously low but the conditions of work generally pleasant and the pace of operations leisurely. Her employers and their families were devoted to her. From the early 1920s she was secretary to a noted admiralty lawyer. Upon his death from tuberculosis in the late 1930s his widow, in gratitude for Dora's longtime fidelity and help, presented her with a magnificent fur coat that she could never have thought of buying for herself. She was legal guardian for two of their children.

As the years went by, Dora became something of a Charleston character. Utterly without social ambition, she drew her numerous friendships from all elements. She was disorganized, helter-skelter in her ways. Her apartment was always stacked high with newspapers that she hadn't been able to get around to reading yet. Her commodious purse, bulging at the seams, was a family joke. Yet with her secretarial work she was scrupulously meticulous. She proved adept with figures, and for many years, until well after she retired from work, she regularly prepared the income tax reports for her former employer's family and various friends, declining to accept compensation.

On Broad Street in the 1920s, 1930s, and 1940s, the workday for employers and clerical personnel was, in effect, divided into two segments. People arrived at the office at 8:30 or 9 A.M., worked until 1:30 or 2 P.M., then went home for early afternoon dinner, returning to the office and working until 6. It was a six-day work week. On Saturdays they did not go back after dinner.

Dora rode the Belt Line trolley car to work. She emerged from the apartment house only at the last minute, and if she was late the motormen on the route would wait at the corner for her to show up.

Her morning walks from her office to the post office and the courthouse were social occasions. She was greeted by numerous acquaintances, chatted briefly with friends up and down the street. When waiting on the corner of Broad and State Streets for the trolley car that would take her home, either for dinner or at the close of the workday, she was more often than not recognized by a passing motorist and given a ride.

Of my three aunts, Dora was much the most interesting. She was born at a time when, even if the family had not been in financial straits, very few women in Southern Jewish (or for that matter, Southern non-Jewish) families were educated beyond high school. In Dora's instance her formal education ended with elementary school. Highly intelligent, she liked to read and to listen to classical music. Her mind, however, was untrained and unfocused; she could not deal with ideas in any sustained way, and her reading was random and scattershot. Her next-younger sister, my Aunt Essie, said once, when Dora was in her eighties, that she always refused to face up to reality. It was a family custom, when I was growing up, to withhold bad news of consequence from her, on the grounds that she would become too greatly upset.

She was in her late forties by the time that I came to know her well, so I always thought of her as middle-aged and older. A snapshot taken in the early 1910s, however, shows her as a quite handsome young woman. Whether she ever came close to marrying, I do not know. It would be hard to imagine that she did not have admirers.

When early in World War II the Broad Street law firm for whom she had worked for several decades underwent a reorganization, Dora applied for a position at the Charleston Navy Yard, which was undergoing massive expansion. She was hired, at a salary more than double her previous earnings. She found herself working, however, for a bureaucrat totally lacking in the manners, courtesies, and amiability that characterized the deferential routines of the downtown legal district. Under such conditions she was unable to function efficiently, and her distress was taken for uncooperativeness.

In those days the nature of psychosomatic responses to stress was only imperfectly understood in the Charleston medical community, so when she developed a rash that spread over her chest and neck, causing irritation and itching, a succession of salves and medicines was prescribed. Finally it was decided that Dora's affliction was due to "nerves," and she was encouraged to give up her job at the Navy Yard and return to the more well-mannered and gentlemanly, if considerably less remunerative, employer-employee relationships of Broad Street. To make it possible, her brothers provided a supplement to her income.

So she went back to the legal and financial district, the rash disappeared, and she worked as secretary to several young attorneys in succession, retiring finally in the early 1960s. She knew everybody on Broad Street, having been employed there, except for two brief interludes, for a half-century. Early in her tenure, in 1908 before the historical zoning ordinance had been enacted, the People's Bank Building, eight stories high, was erected at Broad and State Streets. It was referred to at the time as "the skyscraper." For the remainder of her life Dora called it that. When she retired, admiring friends in the Charleston legal profession presented her with a silver service.

While in her fifties she startled her friends by enrolling in Miss Mamie Forbes's class in tap dancing. Thereafter, until well into her eighties, upon the slightest occasion for celebration she would break into a dance. In the 1950s and 1960s she enjoyed her occasional visits to my parents in Richmond, four hundred miles away. Her trips there and back to Charleston aboard the Atlantic Coast Line's Havana Special were social expeditions. Long before she arrived at her destination she was on good terms with all passengers seated nearby, and the conductor and porter were looking out for her comfort and well-being. In Richmond she delighted in going downtown to shop in the department stores, which were considerably larger than those in Charleston. "Me for the escalators!" she announced as she prepared to set out for Miller & Rhoads and Thalhimer's.

The apartment house where she lived, overlooking the Colonial Lake and owned by a family friend, Marguerite Murphy, was in effect a form of communal living, for almost everyone knew almost everyone else, and there was a constant procession of residents dropping in on each other. When she moved into an apartment by herself in the late 1920s she learned to cook, and became quite proficient at it. As a youth I liked to sit out on the balcony of her apartment, watch her arrive from work on the trolley car, and time how long it would take for her to make her way up to the third floor. With halts and pauses en route to talk with friends, her ascent often took ten minutes or longer. Often I accompanied her to concerts and to plays at the Dock Street Theater. I enjoyed the performances and being with her but found it embarrassing to be introduced to so many people; almost everyone seemed to know her.

She had a marvelous sense of humor and a ready interest in the doings of others. She liked having her brothers tease her, and I quickly fell into the same relationship. As noted, she enjoyed jokes about her age, and also her weight—she was not fat, she insisted (as indeed she was not), only "stylishly plump." Once, while in the Army during World War II, I visited the Washington Zoo and sent her a postcard picturing a hippopotamus. "Thinking of you," I wrote on it. She carried it around in her pocketbook to show her friends. We also had a continuing joke centering on the generous dimensions of steamships. "It's your last ride, Titanic," I would caution her, "fare thee well!"

Once in the late 1970s when there were mild earthquake tremors reported in Charleston, I telephoned her and asked whether she had felt them. Yes, she said, she had.

"Was it as bad as the last time?" I asked her, referring to the 1886 Charleston Earthquake, which occurred about two years before she was born.

"You go to hell!" she declared.

Late in her life there was a conversation in which someone remarked that when the Roman Catholic cathedral nearby had been rebuilt in the early 1900s the steeple had never been completed. "Why not?" she demanded suddenly, having heard what preceded only imperfectly, as old people sometimes do. I was an amateur printer, and when I got home I printed up some Vatican letterhead, in two colors with a crucifix, and wrote a letter to her, asking her whether she could shed light on why the steeple of the Cathedral of St. John the Baptist in Charleston had never been completed, being almost the only person who might remember the circumstances of its construction. I signed it John Paul II. This delighted her.

In the late 1960s, after Marguerite Murphy's death, the Berkeley Court Apartments were allowed to grow unacceptably rundown, and she and her two sisters moved to a new apartment house overlooking the Ashley River. In good weather she spent much of the day on a balcony watching the marine activity. I bought her a pair of binoculars, and the son of her longtime employer, a Merchant Marine officer, gave her a battery-operated marine radio so that she could listen to the conversations between the ships and tugboats. By then my two bachelor uncles, Dan and Manning, had died, and had left their estates to the three aunts, so that they were reasonably well fixed and no longer had to worry about money.

In the late 1980s she fell and broke her hip. Although she said she had momentarily lost her balance, it is possible that she had suffered a brief stroke. Amid the indignities of having to be cared for, she remained cheerful. For a while it was necessary for her to use a bedpan; she declared she was changing her name from Dora to Pandora.

One of the practical nurses who looked after her during her last years amused her greatly by reciting for her diversion a poem:

> *Lord have mercy on my soul*
> *For the chickens I have stole*
> *Two last night and two the night before*
> *Going back tonight and get four more*

Dora quoted it verbatim thereafter.

She continued to read, in particular her favorite novel, *Pride and Prejudice,* and the Old and New Testaments. Her sisters expressed their puzzlement at the last-named, for she was a devout Jew, or Jewess as she termed it. I assured her that given her record, she was wise to overlook no bets. That amused her very much.

When she was ninety-one, another Dora Rubin, no relation, who had once lived in Charleston, died and was buried in the Jewish cemetery to the north of the city. A friend of mine, Elizabeth Hamilton, whose mother, the painter Elizabeth O'Neill Verner, had been a good friend of my Aunt Dora's, read the funeral notice in the local paper, sent flowers, and showed up for the graveside services. Not finding me there, she hurried back and called long distance to find out why I had not been in attendance. I happened to be out of town, and my wife, who received the call, was perplexed; she had heard nothing about Dora's having died. Betty then telephoned my aunts' residence and discovered her mistake. When I returned home I called Dora. The next time she died, I told her, she must make sure to do it properly, because Betty Hamilton couldn't afford to keep sending flowers like that. She laughed delightedly, which by then she did not do very often, my aunts said.

Toward the very end she did want to die. She lost, finally, the ability to sustain the cheerfulness that had helped see her through so many rough times. In the last months of her life she refused all food and dwindled down to almost birdlike weight. Her features had lost their accustomed fullness, and now, little more than skin and bones, her face bore the lean, high-cheeked, almost hawklike appearance of her father—the primal visage of our family—with the deep-socketed eyes now closed tightly.

She was ninety-four years old when she died and was buried alongside her parents and her brothers. Hundreds of relatives and friends gathered at the cemetery to pay their last respects. "It's your last ride, Titanic, fare thee well!" I whispered to her when I walked past her flower-heaped coffin.

3

The Patriarch

MY UNCLE HARRY, WHO was given to striking poses, was holding forth at dinner one day about the ideal existence. "If I could have lived at any time and in any place I chose," he declared expansively, "I'd like to have been a citizen of Charleston in the year 1810."

To which my Uncle Manning, a man of quick wit, responded, "All right, but when you go to the hospital with yellow fever, don't expect me to come to see you."

The exchange was characteristic of both of them. Harry's view of Charleston and the Old South was steeped in the local pieties; Manning was a confirmed skeptic. Of my father's brothers, Harry was the one I knew least well. Short in stature, with large, luminous eyes and prominent cheekbones, he resembled closely what I believe my grandfather would have looked like, without the moustache. As the oldest son, when my grandparents became ill he became in effect the family's principal breadwinner, and thereafter assumed the role of patriarch. By the time I came to know him, which was when he was in his fifties, the sense that he was sitting in judgment was enhanced by his deafness. At all times he wore an earphone wired to an electric amplifier in his pocket. I did not have conversations with him, so much as audiences. He took care to observe the proprieties. Coat and tie were always worn, and he did not ever venture upon the street without a hat.

He liked to think of himself as a cosmopolitan. The first time I took my wife down to Charleston to meet my uncles and aunts, he proposed to mix martinis. "Oh, I know how to make 'em," he assured me.

"How do you make them?" I asked him.

"You mix two parts gin, one part dry vermouth, and add an olive."

"I thought it was more like three to one," I said. (I might have added, but did not, that we had friends in Baltimore who preferred four and even five to one.)

Harry shook his head. "Mighty strong," he declared.

Like the others in the family he had a sense of humor, which in his instance took the form of little mocking parodies that he wrote and ironic jokes he sometimes told. Always, however, there was a political edge to them, for he was an archconservative, and little that took place in government from the early days of the New Deal onward met with his approval. When the civil rights movement began developing in the 1940s he grew obsessed with the subject, and it became difficult to converse with him without the supposed iniquities of the advocates of racial integration dominating his talk.

He was highly intelligent, with an incipient intellectual and even literary bent which under different and better auspices might have eventuated in a more interesting career than the one he pursued. He told me that he was once offered a position as a reporter on the *Morning News* of Savannah, Georgia. I daresay he would have done well in journalism, for the letters to the editor which he contributed regularly to the *Charleston News and Courier* were crisply worded and to the point. Had he become a newspaperman, as two of his brothers did, and as he grew older taken to writing editorials, he would have made all too exemplary a spokesman for the recalcitrant political and social attitudes of Lowcountry cities such as Savannah and Charleston.

As it was, he worked throughout his life for a wholesale dry goods house, M. Hornik and Co. In later years he was a partner in the firm, but his income was never large. His son, my cousin Harry, Jr., said that he did not really like his work. Yet he went to the office five days a week and Saturday mornings, and usually for several hours on Sunday morning as well.

Why he did not accept the invitation to join the newspaper staff, which I assume was made in the 1920s when he was living in Savannah, probably had to do with the element of risk that venturing upon a new occupation would have posed. He was married by then, with a son. There was little in his early life that would have encouraged him to take chances. Born in Charleston in 1889, he was in his early teens when his father became ill and unable to provide for the family. He went to work as a stock boy at what could only have been very low wages, saw his brothers sent away to a home for orphans and dependent upon charity, and experienced the humiliation of knowing that others were only too well aware of the family's indigence and need.

When finally he achieved a measure of stability and respectability, he would not jeopardize his hard-won status. His position with the dry goods firm was secure, and his earnings, while modest, were adequate. To set aside that security in order to try a new vocation, however more interesting and potentially to his taste, was to take a greater gamble than he could accept.

The element of respectability played a central role in defining Harry's life and character. The heavy responsibilities that were thrust upon him as a youth, the need to preside over a household of which the youngest child was no more than a couple of years old, impelled him to assume a preternatural severity of outlook and bearing. In his dealings with the world there would have been every incentive to exhibit his seriousness of purpose, to demonstrate to others—and to himself as well—his probity and trustworthiness. As a young Jew, the son of an immigrant father, he sought to make his way in a community in which financial power lay with the old families. There could be, for him, abundant reason to merit the good opinion of those in positions of authority. The lares and penates were to be faithfully observed and honored.

Not surprisingly, Harry's response, once he had begun to establish himself, was to take the local pieties for his own. It was not that he sought to ingratiate himself with the gentry, for so far as I know he was without social ambition. It was rather that he accepted their ideals and values, and lived his life accordingly. It was not prestige that he wanted, but good opinions.

He liked to read. He read mainly books of history—more particularly, Southern history. His approach was not that of the scholar but the
votary; he read in order to confirm and to rehearse the community
verities. Once he remarked to me that his name would go down in history. For proof he showed me a two-volume edition of Jefferson Davis's
The Rise and Fall of the Confederate Government, published in the 1920s
by the United Daughters of the Confederacy, with his name listed
among the subscribers. On the surface this was a joke—literally, his
name did appear in a historical work. But what he was also demonstrating was that he was among those patriotic Southerners who were
sponsors of the wartime president's account of the War for Southern
Independence. I doubt that he actually read the two-volume work himself, although he may have dipped into it. A dreary rehearsal of Davis's
version of what happened, it is composed in a style as dry and un-
bending as was the author himself.

The person Harry admired almost to idolatry was the editor of the
News and Courier, William Watts Ball, an old-school Southern journalist. Ball possessed an epigrammatical style and a combativeness that
made him the ideal spokesman for Southern diehards. Author of a
controversial memoir entitled *The State That Forgot: South Carolina's
Surrender to Democracy,* Ball believed firmly in government by the Better Sort and had little use for social amelioration. As might be expected, the innovative programs of the New Deal that were developed
to break the grip of the economic depression of the early 1930s were
not to his editorial liking. Within two years of the election of Franklin
D. Roosevelt, Ball was hammering away at the Democratic administration, labor unions, social security, public works programs to provide
jobs for the unemployed, federal farm subsidies, antitrust prosecutions
of utilities monopolies—all these, and more besides, were baleful mile-
stones on the road to socialism.

In the social programs of the New Deal, Ball was quick to spot a
threat to Southern racial arrangements, and the *News and Courier's* editorial page openly championed the cause of white supremacy, repeat-
edly issuing stern warnings of the danger of "Negro rule." As might be

expected, such views received widespread acceptance among the members of the Charleston establishment.

They were assuredly my Uncle Harry's convictions. Like not a few of his fellow citizens, he prided himself on his intransigence. Historically Charlestonians were known for their penchant for taking extreme positions. As Nullificationists and then Secessionists, they delighted in demonstrating to one another the extravagance of their political and social attitudes.

It is interesting that not only Uncle Harry but, on a more prestigious civic level, William Watts Ball himself were not born into the Charleston establishment but were, in a sense, converts. In a community whose social elite prided themselves on their descent from the planter families of the Carolina Lowcountry during the colonial and early national era, Ball was from Upcountry South Carolina, and married into the Lowcountry gentry. As frequently happens, it is the newcomers who can best articulate the attitudes and values of the group whose ranks they join, since they do not take such things for granted but consciously enunciate and objectify them.

The Old South, with its aristocratic ideal and its martial bearing, was Uncle Harry's Eldorado. His ideological and political stances were exaggerated to the point of absurdity, with the element of pose all too obvious. In the early 1950s I brought my wife to visit the family in Charleston for the first time, and since she was Northern-born and studying for a doctoral degree in political science at Johns Hopkins, Harry felt it incumbent to demonstrate both his sophistication and his recalcitrance, suspecting rightly that she was a political liberal. I had warned her what to expect, and she took care not to argue with him, however extravagant the views he might express. Suffice it to say that he lived up to my expectations.

The bane of Harry's existence—and that of W. W. Ball and numerous other political conservatives as well—was Eleanor Roosevelt. The First Lady's liberalism, her activism, her outspoken belief in equality of opportunity and government intervention in support of the downtrodden, and the ubiquity with which she turned up everywhere to champion her cause were constant sources of exasperation. Yet oddly enough, there were aspects in which Harry's wife, my Aunt Ruth, resembled Mrs. Roosevelt—though not in her political beliefs.

A remarkable woman, Ruth Ensel Rubin was the daughter of an antebellum Jewish family in Savannah, where she had been a member of Juliette Low's pioneer Girl Scouts of America troop and graduated from junior college there. She was highly efficient, an articulate speaker, played an active role in numerous civic organizations, held national office in the Council of Jewish Women, and was frequently in the local news.

Charleston was a very self-conscious city, and extolling its heritage was an important civic activity. Ruth became active as a volunteer tourist guide. She learned all the historical dates and "firsts" (there was even a first haberdashery store in America on Broad Street), could recite the statistical claims, and took satisfaction in guiding visitors around the old downtown city. This was not social aggrandizement; she and Harry were not party-goers. It was her way of asserting her membership in the community.

Nowadays her intelligence, energy, and efficiency would doubtless have led her in the direction of a successful professional career. As it was, she subordinated her civic activities to her responsibilities as a wife and homemaker; her husband's needs and interests always came first. At the same time she was a considerable "manager" and was adept at arranging matters behind the scenes.

In truth they seemed an odd combination. Ruth was outgoing, perceptive, energetic, something of a "do-gooder," who certainly believed in improving the shining hour. In another place and under other circumstances, she would have been an active advocate for civic, social, and racial betterment. She was kindhearted, generous; she took an interest in people, understood other people's points of view. Harry, by contrast, was self-absorbed, not a joiner, and a pessimist about the chances for reform and amelioration of the human condition. Yet theirs was a happy marriage, satisfying to both. During their courtship they exchanged soft-leather-bound editions of the *Rubaíyát*; Harry's to Ruth was inscribed to "Columbine."

I have the sense that, for whatever reason, Ruth very much needed to feel herself not only useful but even indispensable to a husband and a family of her own. In a very basic way, she wished to be the person who was responsible for the comfort, well-being, and proper functioning of her husband and family. She catered to Harry's whims, flattered his self-esteem, indulged his eccentricities, and enabled him to feel not only appreciated but important.

In a sense this was a method of control; that is, it enabled her to use her husband's need to feel himself a Person of Consequence in order to guide his conduct. She saw herself as the farsighted one, the person who gave direction and made the decisions, but through being able to suggest and to steer—by indirection rather than overt assertion. And indeed she *was* level-headed and farsighted, and she did value and cherish her husband's integrity and intelligence, and took delight in his assertiveness, while also determinedly seeing to it that things went as she thought best.

She took responsibility not only for her husband and their son, but for her husband's family as well. When I was a youth she was the only member of the family in Charleston with whom I could talk about much that was important to me. She looked after my three aunts, and in particular Dora. Uncle Manning lived with Harry and Ruth, with a suite of his own. When Dan came back to Charleston on visits, he stayed with them. Manning had oddly spartan tastes in food, and Ruth catered to them. She always made much of the ways of "male Rubins," as she liked to put it. They each had their eccentricities, their seemingly inexplicable tastes and attitudes.

In truth each of the four brothers did have his oddities, but in retrospect there was something of an element of strategy, probably unconsciously so, in her response. For in being treated by her as unique, inscrutable creatures, they were at the same time being locked into their roles. There were certain things they were supposed to like and to dislike, do and not do, and so long as their eccentricities and tastes were

properly observed, they were expected to follow the prescribed behavior.

In any event, Ruth's mode of deference was very much to Uncle
Harry's liking, and he did take satisfaction indeed in being treated as
being singular, preeminent, a law unto himself—when in fact he was
highly conscious of what the Better Sort might think of him, and anx-
ious to be perceived as an adherent of the community loyalties and
pieties.

As might be expected, their only child, my cousin Harry, Jr., two years
older than me, was kept to a severe standard. Highly intelligent, capable, he was encouraged to suppress his emotions, to keep his own
counsel. He attended The Citadel, the Military College of South Carolina, where he won advanced military rank in the corps of cadets. He
graduated in June of 1942, was commissioned in the Marine Corps, and
spent the balance of World War II in the Southwest Pacific. Afterward
he was stationed at Quantico, near Washington, with the rank of captain, and I believe he considered remaining in the Marines as a career.

I remember a newspaper photograph that seems to me to say much
about him. In commemoration of the firing, by cadets of The Citadel,
upon the relief steamer *Star of the West,* which had attempted to re-
supply the beleaguered Union garrison at Fort Sumter on January 5,
1861, there was a ceremonial flag raising and cannon firing near the site
of the wartime harbor battery position. My cousin, who was one of the
party, is shown standing at attention, his body rigidly erect, his face
stern and features severe, in the best martial ideal—as if engaged in
playing a role.

I should not be surprised if his parents did not encourage the idea
of his becoming a career Marine officer. Certainly it would have
pleased his father very much; few roles were more respected in
Charleston than that of an officer and a gentleman. For her part, his
mother, knowing that he was shy and self-conscious in the presence of
girls, had a future wife picked out for him, in the person of a cousin.
She went so far as to communicate this to the intended. There was

even, I understand, an engagement ring which had belonged to Ruth's own grandmother, and which Harry, Jr., was to use when proposing.

It never came to that. The intended developed other plans. My cousin enrolled in law school, met and married a girl from upstate South Carolina who was employed as a journalist in Washington. Thereafter his life took a very different turn. He began to break out of the rigid, emotionally cramped pattern to which he had sought to conform, and to discover a warmer, more congenial way of living.

Not too long after the engagement was announced, I was in Charleston, and Ruth was telling me about how, some months before, she had known that something was afoot. She had needed to talk to my cousin about something, and when he did not answer his telephone, she had found a number on a piece of paper in some clothes he had left in Charleston, and called it. It was his future wife's telephone number, and my cousin was there. Knowing my cousin as I did, it occurred to me that, short of dire emergency, it must have been extremely embarrassing to him to have his mother call him at that number.

It was not that Aunt Ruth or Uncle Harry desired to dominate their son's life. But Uncle Harry had built so many barriers to protect himself against the intrusion of chaos, and Ruth was so eager to see to it that their son's pathway was surefooted and free of missteps, that in retrospect it was almost inevitable that my cousin would insist upon choosing his own route. It was also inevitable that his bride would quickly identify his mother's urge to share in his life, and there would be resentment and hostility, the more so because her political and social attitudes were so different from those of his family.

Uncle Harry's dislike and distrust of Franklin D. Roosevelt and the New Deal can be indicated by a display he assembled. He secured a set of portraits and photographs of the presidents of the United States and mounted them in a large glass picture frame, which he placed on the wall of his living room. All were there, as well as Jefferson Davis for the Civil War years, with a legend under each listing their accomplishments, and with portraits of uniform size. The one exception was FDR;

his picture was far smaller than the others, and the space alongside and beneath it was filled with a catalog of his crimes.

During the 1940s and 1950s, as civil rights increasingly became a major issue, Harry's views grew ever more compulsively reactionary. As might be expected, he was militantly anti-Communist and did not hesitate to equate political liberalism with socialism, which for him was tantamount to subversion. When in the late 1940s Joseph McCarthy began making headlines with his denunciations of supposed Communists in government, Harry was very much on the Wisconsin senator's side.

For the last several years of his life he was bedridden from nerves damaged in an operation. In his bedroom upstairs he listened to the radio news, and it was his habit to deliver his own commentary on it in a voice loud enough that anyone who might be downstairs could hear him. In the early 1950s I happened to be on hand when the midday news program by Paul Harvey came over the radio. Harvey's politics were decidedly on the conservative side, and his method of expressing them highly flamboyant. Harry always waited eagerly to hear Harvey's interpretation of events, which he would supplement with his own interpolated comments.

On this particular occasion, however, McCarthy's latest tactics had proved too flagrantly irresponsible not only for the Democrats but for influential Republicans as well, and instead of voicing his customary approval of the senator's brand of reckless anti-Communism, Harvey felt obliged to censure him.

I listened to the radio playing upstairs and waited to hear what the response would be to this surprising and totally unprecedented chastisement of McCarthy by my uncle's favorite radio commentator. There was a long silence before Harry delivered his verdict.

"That's what *he* says," he announced at last.

Harry's political and social views were so strongly held and obsessively enunciated, and so relatively crude in the form of expression they took, that it is scarcely an exaggeration to describe them as being close to pathological. He became in effect a kind of Professional Southerner, taking pride in demonstrating how intemperate, from the standpoint of national (though not of Charleston) opinion, he could be.

There was a xenophobic aspect to his attitudes, and a suggestion of Jewish anti-Semitism, for he came to equate Jews from New York City and the Northeast with the assertion of liberal political views. It was all too obvious that, without ever examining his own motives, he perceived in the public role of Jewish liberals an implied threat to his own status within the community. On occasions when he was in the company of the rabbi of K. K. Beth Elohim, as sometimes happened because of Ruth's active involvement in the temple's affairs, he did not hesitate to make his opinions known.

Harry was by no means the only political conservative in the family. His next-younger brother, my Uncle Dan, was of a similar mind. Dan, who left Charleston while still in his teens and never returned there to live, was likewise opposed to what he considered the fiscal irresponsibility and charlatanism of liberal politicians, and fully believed every Democratic administration from the New Deal onward to be "soft on Communism." Yet much though Dan and I disagreed on politics—and he would sometimes become so angry at my liberal views that he would leave off writing to me for months at a time—I never had the sense that his conservatism involved posturing or attitudinizing. He was not intent upon demonstrating his community credentials or asserting his orthodoxy. With Harry, by contrast, there was always the feeling that he had something to prove, and that the intensity with which he sounded off on matters of politics and race was, as with his insistence upon never going outside without being clad in hat, coat, and necktie, a way of attesting to his gentlemanly respectability.

Harry was greatly pleased when in his late fifties he was elected to membership in the Charleston Club, on East Bay Street. So far as I know he was without any particular need for the facilities of a club, for he did not play cards, dine out, or sit around drinking. That, however, was not the point. An organization formed for social purposes by conservative Charlestonians, mainly businessmen and professional men, had invited him to become a member. "There's one place I can go," he told me proudly, "where I don't have to listen to liberal talk!" I am glad, for his sake, that he did gain a measure at least of the particular kind of respectability that was so important to him.

It would be nice to be able to say that the late years of his life were more satisfying, but quite the opposite was true. In the early 1950s he came down with tuberculosis. An operation on his lungs resulted in damage to certain nerves which, as he grew old, caused increasing pain. By the mid-1950s he was permanently invalided.

What happened next was catastrophic. In 1957 his son, my cousin Harry, Jr., then a young lawyer in Washington, developed an obscure but virulent muscular disease, probably contracted during his wartime service in the Pacific, and died at age thirty-six, leaving a wife and three small children. There had always been tension between Ruth and her daughter-in-law, who now with her straitened finances found it necessary to move back with her own parents in Upcountry South Carolina. Though not as outgoing as Ruth, she too was strong-willed. I doubt that, given the personalities involved, anything could have made the relationship go well. Without my cousin to mediate, it was not long before his widow proceeded to sever all relations with his family, and declined to bring her children to see their father's parents or to invite their grandmother to visit them. Ruth died in 1963 without ever seeing them again, three years after my Uncle Harry's death and six after her only son's.

My aunts were indignant over my cousin's widow's refusal to maintain any ties. Not only were they upset for Ruth's sake, but they had loved my cousin, and not to be allowed to know his little children was a keen deprivation. My assumption is that the emotional shock of my cousin's death and its consequences remained so devastating that his widow could not bear to keep up contact with his mother and family. It was not a matter for resentment or blame. It was a tragedy, for everyone concerned. Good people, decent, cruelly bereaved, were caught in a heartbreaking predicament. There was a rift, which my cousin's untimely death deepened into a chasm. It could not be bridged.

To return to the family's early years, it seems to me that of all of the children of Hyman Levy and Fannie Sanders Rubin, my Uncle Harry was the most punished by those times of poverty and mortification. Responsibilities were thrust upon him early on. It is difficult even to think of him as a small child, without a burden to bear. The dread of insecurity and the desire for respectability came to dominate his mind. Change and innovation were seen as menacing his modest, hard-won status. He drew in his boundaries and constricted his sympathies, thereby excluding much of the possibilities for joy. The ill fortune that dogged his younger days was renewed at the close, with stored-up intensity. In a family chronicle that includes no small portion of blight, Harry's story, I think, is the saddest of all.

4

Riddle Me This

ALONE OF THE FOUR BROTHERS, my Uncle Dan, next oldest to Harry, left Charleston as a young man. While working as a newspaperman he taught himself to write plays. When in his thirties he had five new plays on Broadway in seven years, then spent a half-dozen years in Hollywood writing movie scripts for Paramount Studios. Resuming his playwriting, during the last quarter-century of his life he wrote two new plays each year. Not one of them was ever produced.

When at work on a play he went into seclusion for several months at a time. Other than what was absolutely necessary he wrote no letters, saw nobody, read only the daily newspaper. He approached a dramatic situation as if he were solving a problem, thinking it out until he worked out his plot, then put the words on paper. His need—and ability—to concentrate his attention on the play he was writing went beyond ordinary engrossment; it was a total immersion of intellect and emotion in the act of imagining. He existed in a vacuum, so to speak, in which human relationships, physical surroundings, what went on about him virtually ceased to command his attention. He lived in hotels, and in order to achieve his concentration on what he was writing he required quiet; when he could not escape the sound of a radio playing, he changed his lodgings.

Like Harry he grew politically obsessed as the years went by. Once, as a joke, I told him that when he died, instead of a rabbi conducting the services I intended to ask U.S. Senator Barry Goldwater, the ranking conservative politician of the time, to do it. That would be fine with him, he said, without so much as a trace of a smile. The parlous state of the nation, as he saw it, was no laughing matter.

As noted earlier, much though I disagreed with his political opinions I did not have the sense that Dan's ultraconservatism was impelled by a wish to be identified by others as one who held sound views. Unlike what may have been true of my Uncle Harry, the desire for status and respectability was not a fetish with Dan. If there was a compulsion at work—and I think there was—it had to do with the need to be free of any kind of dependence upon others, and a corresponding distrust of schemes for social betterment and amelioration of poverty.

Spare in stature, firm-jawed, with an angular, bony face, he had tremendous willpower, and on occasion a formidable temper. As a young newspaperman he had set his sights upon becoming a playwright, and to do so he was willing to sacrifice comfort, leisure, convenience, possessions, companionship—whatever was necessary to achieve his objective. He learned to divide his day into two days, he told me. He did his newspaper work, got some exercise at the YMCA, slept for several hours. Then he worked at his playwriting, followed by another four hours of sleep.

He never married, did not accumulate possessions, lived alone in hotels. If he was lonely, he would not concede it, even to himself. Throughout his life he would concede little or nothing. Having learned early on that he could not depend upon the help of others, thereafter he relied upon his own resolve.

Of my three uncles, he was the one with whom I was closest. From my early teens on, we corresponded regularly. For the last eighteen years, until his death in 1965, he lived in El Paso, Texas. I went out to visit him several times. Previous to that he lived in New York, and before that in California. Every several years he paid two-week visits to Charleston.

His was born in Charleston in 1892. When his parents grew ill and he and his two younger brothers were sent to stay at the Hebrew Orphans' Home in Atlanta, he was ten years old. That Dan much resented being sent to the orphanage I feel quite sure, but I doubt that he would ever have allowed himself to complain about it, even to his brothers. He would have loathed having anyone give the slightest sign of feeling sorry for him. If when he attended school in Atlanta a schoolmate ever made so bold as to intimate any contempt for his situation, his response would have been swift and violent.

When he reached the age of twelve and completed elementary school, he was allowed to return to Charleston and look for work. His two younger brothers followed a year later. Dan found a job as an office boy at a wholesale paper company. The family's poverty, and the consciousness that it was known to others, rankled. His father's ineffectiveness as a merchant, and what I suspect Dan may have considered his too-ready acquiescence in his condition, very likely exasperated his son. My father told me that when Hyman Levy Rubin died late in 1911, Dan, who was then living and working in Birmingham, Alabama, was not on speaking terms with his father. My aunts denied this, but my hunch is that my father knew whereof he spoke.

Dan's aspiration was to write, and as was true for many an ambitious youth during the late nineteenth and early twentieth centuries, the avenue to a literary vocation was through newspaper writing. There was an opening on the staff of the morning newspaper in Charleston, the *News and Courier,* and Dan and another young man applied for it. The arrangement was that they would work for three months without salary, I assume at space rates, after which the one who performed better would receive a job as a reporter—at a salary of five dollars a week.

Dan's rival was a college graduate, and for all that Dan read and studied avidly, the disparity in educational background at the time was too great to be overcome. At the conclusion of the trial period the position went to his rival. The editor was impressed with Dan's abilities, however, and when a newspaper in Birmingham announced over the Associated Press wire that there was a vacancy on its staff, Dan was recommended for it. He was given the job, and at the age of seventeen or eighteen he left Charleston.

Until the early 1920s he worked as a newsman in Birmingham, with time out for military service during the war, then moved on to newspapers in Denver, Fort Worth, Jacksonville, and Columbia, South Carolina. That he must have been good at the trade may be gathered from something that happened decades later. In 1947 I applied for a position on the Norfolk, Virginia, *Ledger-Dispatch*. The managing editor wrote back to say that he had no vacancies on the staff just then. Noting, however, that I had listed my birthplace as Charleston, South Carolina, he asked whether I happened to be related to a Daniel Rubin who once worked on a newspaper in Birmingham. "Anyone related to that Dan Rubin would have to be worth his weight in gold in a newsroom," he declared.

There were others on the staff of the Birmingham newspapers who entertained literary ambitions, among them Dan's childhood friend Octavus Roy Cohen, who was beginning to publish fiction in the magazines. A group began meeting together each week to read and discuss each others' writings.

Why Dan chose to pursue playwriting rather than fiction, I do not know. He remarked once that all he could write was dialogue. In any event, he read every play he could get his hands on, and as a reporter was no doubt able to get passes to attend the plays that came through Birmingham on the stock company circuit.

His hopes of becoming a playwright were suspended when the United States entered the First World War. Despite the fact that he had only a seventh-grade education, Dan determined to apply for an officer's commission. Here again his willpower exerted itself. To qualify for officers' training school it was necessary to demonstrate competence in trigonometry. He got hold of a textbook and taught himself enough to pass the examination. He was commissioned a second lieutenant and assigned to the 327th Infantry Regiment, part of the 82nd Division.

I have wondered sometimes what the enlisted men in his platoon, most of them from the small-town and rural South, must have thought when they first encountered this small, lightly built young Jew, wearing second lieutenant's bars and a Sam Browne belt, who had been assigned to lead them in battle. It would not have taken very long for them to discover that for all his slight stature he was thoroughly capable of handling whatever was expected in the way of lengthy marches and rigorous physical conditioning and training. He meant business; they would quickly have realized that.

He once described to me an incident in France when the troops in his division were being tutored in trench warfare by an English noncom. As was customary in the British Army but not permitted in ours, the NCO did a great deal of cursing and swearing at his pupils when monitoring their actions. After holding forth on the way to use the bayonet in combat, he started in on the aiming and firing of rifles, insisting upon the English method, and belaboring his audience for their supposed stupidity in failing to follow his directions. Most of the Americans were from small towns or the Southern countryside and had been shooting rifles all their lives. During a pause the men in Dan's platoon, uncertain what to make of the unexpected personal abuse, waited for Dan to say something.

"Men," Dan declared after a moment, with the British NCO standing by listening, "when the British tell you how to handle a bayonet, you listen to what they tell you, because they know what they're talking about. But when they try to tell you how to shoot, you know how to do that for yourselves, so don't pay any attention to them." There was no more trouble from the NCO after that, Dan said.

Dan's unit moved into the front lines in time for the American offensives at St. Mihiel and the Meuse-Argonne. Several days into the latter, during which the 327th suffered heavy casualties, he was kneeling next to a tree to supervise the setting up of a machine gun emplacement when a German shell exploded close by, instantly killing the two men with him. Only the partial shelter of the tree trunk saved his life. As it was, he was severely wounded in the legs and back, and half-buried under earth and debris. A full day and night elapsed before he was discovered and taken by medics to the rear. At the time, he said, he was in shock; only when he was in a hospital train and being taken to a hospital behind the lines did he begin to feel pain.

The war ended not long thereafter, and in the late spring of 1919 he was sent home aboard a hospital ship, which docked at the Charleston Navy Yard; from there he was taken to an Army hospital in Atlanta. Once again he found himself in that city under less than pleasant circumstances.

While there, an incident occurred to which his response was characteristic. As a patriotic gesture a social club, I believe the Piedmont Driving Club, had a policy of writing to all wounded officers hospitalized in Atlanta, inviting them to make use of the club facilities. In due course Dan received such a letter. Knowing that the club did not admit Jews into membership, he wrote back declining the invitation. He would not make use of his military uniform, he told them, to avail himself of a privilege that if he were a civilian would have been denied him because of his religion.

It was the gesture of one for whom any sense of being patronized was intolerable. Personal honor, rigid adherence to principle—these were not to be relaxed. In the mid-1920s, when he was a reporter on the *Jacksonville Floridian,* he was given some information in confidence by a local politician, and he told his editor about it, making it clear that the information was not for publication. The editor published it, whereupon Dan promptly resigned.

The same strict obedience to principle manifested itself in the mid-1930s, when Congress voted to pay a long-delayed bonus to the veterans of the war of 1917–1918. On the grounds that service to one's country in war merited no such largesse, Dan declined to accept it. (My father, who was less given to taking ideological positions, used his bonus money to have a picket fence built around our property.)

After Dan's recovery from his wounds he returned to Birmingham to resume his job as a reporter, and again set out to write plays. His boyhood friend Octavus Roy Cohen had meanwhile begun producing his Florian Slappey stories, which the *Saturday Evening Post* was publishing regularly. The stories, which caricatured black life in what nowadays would be outrageously unacceptable fashion, were widely popular. Cohen's commercial success, Dan found, had gone to his head. At the sessions of the writing group "he was like a king holding court." Dan dropped out.

When he decided that his own dramatic technique had advanced sufficiently to begin looking for a producer, he selected a literary agent at random from the yellow pages of the New York City telephone directory, and sent a play to him. In 1926, while working as the telegraph editor of the *Columbia (S.C.) Record,* he had not one but two plays accepted and produced on Broadway. The first was a quick failure, but the second, *Devils,* had a three-month run, attracted considerable attention, and drew mixed reviews. Percy Hammond, in the *New York Herald-Tribune,* termed it "a courageous and relentless combination of acting and drama, which is something to rave about in this soft season." Brooks Atkinson, in the *New York Times,* reported that at the final curtain the audience "burst into prolonged applause and remained seated for several minutes."

There followed several more Broadway plays, each more successful than its predecessor. *Women Go On Forever,* produced in 1927 and starring Mary Boland and James Cagney, was a considerable hit both in New York and then on tour. Alexander Woollcott in the *New York World* referred to "its salty flavor, its unfamiliar pattern, its imaginative vividness, and its wild, undisciplined miscellaneousness." *Time* magazine's reviewer declared that "it transcends the merely artful and achieves a gritty reality that is truly great." Dan's earnings were such that he was able to quit his newspaper job and devote full time to playwriting.

His most successful play, *Riddle Me This,* produced in 1932, ran for an entire Broadway season. A murder mystery, what made it unusual was that it opened with the murder being committed on stage, so that the audience knew the identity of the killer. Yet as the police investigation developed, what was turned up seemed so convincing that the audience was made almost to discredit what it had seen and to believe that someone else had done it.

Much of the play's attraction lay in the repartee between a police detective and a reporter, who were played by Frank Craven and Thomas Mitchell, two of the era's best-known actors. Whitney Bolton in the *Morning Telegraph* referred to "good performances, a good play, a rarely good idea, and a completely able whole production. It would seem to me to be a hit." Robert Garland in the *World-Telegram* declared that "to my way of thinking, 'Riddle Me This' possesses almost everything needed to create a perfect evening's entertainment. And that everything includes a long and prosperous future." John Mason Brown in the *Evening Post* termed the play "not only the best murder drama the present theater has revealed but one of its most laughable comedies." And so on; this time there were no bad reviews, and the play was featured in cartoons and drawings.

The movie rights were sold, and the film, with Victor McLaglen and Edmund Lowe playing the detective and the reporter, was likewise a considerable success. Later another version was filmed and produced. Published by Samuel French in an actor's edition, for some years thereafter *Riddle Me This* was regularly staged by amateur theater groups.

Dan's Broadway successes led to screenwriting contracts. The late 1920s and the 1930s were his good years. Talkies had only recently come into prominence, and the ability to write crisp dialogue was in demand. He signed a long-term contract with Paramount Studios, where he worked on various scripts. As a child I was once taken down to the Gloria Theater in Charleston and shown Dan's name on a poster in the marquee: "Screen Play by Daniel N. Rubin." The movie was probably *Dishonored,* starring Marlene Dietrich, Victor McLaglen, and Warner Oland, and directed by Josef von Sternberg. Another of his credits was for *The Texans,* with Randolph Scott, Joan Bennett, and May Robson.

It was during his years in Hollywood that Dan came nearest to living what to most people would be thought a "normal" existence. He played golf, spent time with friends. He even purchased a large gray Cadillac, which in the mid-1930s he drove across the continent to Charleston— the one instance I can recall of his ever affecting anything that might be thought of as ostentation. If so, then surely any satisfaction that he took in driving home to Charleston in an expensive automobile was pardonable on the part of one who had been sent away to live in an orphanage and been denied a $5-a-week job as a newspaper reporter after trying out for three months without salary.

He told me that he once came close to getting married, and my guess is that it must have happened during that period. In any event, he decided against it. To marry would be to give hostages to fate; he would no longer be independent of others. Perhaps his thinking went something like this: If he stayed in Hollywood and continued writing movies, he was not only assured of a comfortable income, but could lead the kind of life, with the regular hours and routine, in which there would be a place for domesticity and the permanent company of another human being. If, however, he returned to playwriting, the intensely solitary, self-absorbed regimen that he followed when at work would scarcely be compatible with marriage. Whatever his reasoning may have been, he stayed unmarried.

He did not care for many aspects of the Hollywood milieu. Clearly he was quite competent at the work, as the screen credits he received testify. He not only went to Hollywood at a good salary, but earned at least one sizable raise while there. Even so, in the late 1930s he decided that writing for the movies was not what he wanted to do with the rest of his life. He had set aside enough money in investments to be able to live on the income from them, so he left his job with Paramount, moved to Carmel-by-the-Sea, near San Francisco, and went back to writing plays. Not long after the attack on Pearl Harbor he moved to New York City.

For my sister and brother and myself, Dan was our magical uncle, who lived out in Hollywood among the film stars, writing movies. At Christmas time—like most Reform Jewish families we celebrated Christmas, but solely as a secular holiday—he sent generous checks to my mother for buying us presents; mother used to call him "Uncle Bim," in reference to the multimillionaire uncle in the Andy Gump comic strip. On a visit to Charleston in the early 1930s he purchased bicycles, our first, for all of us. A little later I was collecting pennants, and I wrote him in California asking him to send me a couple. Soon there arrived in the mail a bulky package of expensive pennants from the West Coast colleges and universities.

It was during the war years that I came to know him well. He was living at a hotel on 43rd Street between Broadway and Sixth Avenue, and in the late summer of 1943, after basic infantry training in the Army, I was sent to Yale University for an Italian area and language

program. During the six months of my stay in New Haven I visited
Dan several times. Mostly we sat in his room and talked. He told me
about his experiences in World War I, his years in Hollywood, his
newspaper years. He talked freely and sometimes quite personally
about the family, had much to say about actors, actresses, and the theater. Politics, however, preoccupied him. Liberal politicos and the notion of a "Brave New World" were anathema to him.

In 1945 he moved to Newburgh, New York. After the war was over
and I had finished college, I went to work as a reporter on a newspaper
in Hackensack, New Jersey. Several times I rode up on the train to
spend weekends with him. Not long afterward, in search of a dry climate for his nasal condition, he moved out to El Paso. Meanwhile I had
gone back to Virginia and found a job as city editor of a small morning newspaper in Staunton.

In 1948 I left newspaper work, temporarily as I thought, for a year
of graduate study in creative writing at the Johns Hopkins University.
That winter I wrote a play, set in the South after the Civil War, in which
Southern racial relationships figured prominently. As drama it was
wretched stuff. I sent a copy to Dan, asking him to tell me what he
thought of it. He found a few good things to say about the dialogue,
but he criticized my handling of the plot, which involved such hack-
neyed devices as overheard conversations and the like. It was when it
came to the theme that he laid into me. My depiction of racial relations, he wrote, was akin to a bird fouling its own nest. Like other
Southern-born writers who depicted their native heath in terms of violence, fanaticism, lynchings, and decadence, he said, I was attempting
to exploit the South in order to curry the favor of a Northern audience.

There was doubtless some truth to the charge. Ironically, the best
response I could have made, although I did not know it at the time,
would have been to remind him of the first of his own plays to enjoy a
successful run on Broadway. Produced in 1926 and starring Sylvia Field
and John Cromwell, *Devils* was set in rural Mississippi and was described by Brooks Atkinson in the *New York Times* as follows:

With the production of Daniel N. Rubin's "Devils," at Maxine Elliott's last evening, "morbid realism," heretofore the special property of the gaunt outcorners of New England, stepped vigorously south to Joel Given's "place" in the Lower Mississippi Valley. In his portrayal of the festers of human living in that backwoods community, Mr. Rubin piled the horrors deep—paternal brutality, religious fanaticism, canine slaughter, betrayal, suicide, all garnished lavishly with a malignant cruelty in personal relations.

The playbill had made the point even more explicitly:

> In the many isolated farming communities in the "backwoods" country of the South the people are intellectually starved, emotionally frustrated, but spiritually self-contained. Two forces dominate them—the cotton crop and religion. Cotton is king, but religion is master, and it is a religion of fear and vengeance, with the Bible taken literally, word for word. It is a rich ground for the seed of fanaticism and intolerance, and with their emotional life so twisted and ill-expressed, the fruit of the seed flourishes.

In any event, I conducted no further forays into the writing of plays. Our correspondence continued unabated, but I did not see Dan again until the mid-1950s when, en route by train from New Orleans to Los Angeles, I stopped over in El Paso for a visit. He was living in a small, undistinguished hotel. I spent several days with him. I had become interested in family history, and I questioned him about my grandparents and the period when he and my father and my other uncles and aunts were growing up in Charleston. I learned little that I did not already know. It was not so much that he was reticent or reluctant, as that he did not appear to recall many details. In retrospect I think that if I had kept asking him about particulars he would probably have remembered and been able to tell me considerably more about my grandparents. Regrettably I did not persist with my inquiry.

I visited him once again in 1963, flying out to El Paso and spending several days with him. He was still in the same hotel. By then he was in his early seventies; his eyes were giving trouble and he had been ordered by his doctors to cut down severely on his reading, so he had bought a phonograph and several dozen long-playing records. (At no time did Dan ever own a radio or a television set.) As we sat in his room talking, occasionally he would glance at a slip of paper, on which, he said, he had noted certain things he wanted to tell me. He must have been anticipating my visit for days, and thinking of what we might talk about.

The hotel was a small walk-up establishment without lobby or front desk, scarcely more than a rooming house. Dan's room was furnished only plainly. His only addition to the furniture was a reclining reading chair, which he insisted that I try out. I wondered whether he was in financial need, but when we went out to a restaurant for dinner and I attempted to pick up the check, he would not let me. "I can afford this better than you," he told me. After a while I decided that if not wealthy he was financially comfortable. (After his death his estate bore out my surmise.) He chose to live as he did because, except during that one period of several years when he lived near the ocean in Carmel, he had resolved to spend no money merely on surroundings. He had also determined not to accumulate possessions beyond his immediate needs. There was not even a shelf of books in his room; the public library provided him with his reading. A typewriter and paper, clothes, a couple of reference works—these were all he required. His one indulgence was cigars, which he bought by the box and chain-smoked; in the last years of his life, at his physician's insistence, he gave them up.

We talked for several days. Not only was he up to date on the doings of the family and their friends in Charleston and elsewhere, but he told me various things that until then I had never known, including some scandalous items, as well as several stories about his young manhood that were by no means flattering to himself. I was impressed with how closely he kept up with the family's doings.

I tried to persuade him to schedule a stop in Roanoke, Virginia, where I was teaching at Hollins College, on his next trip to Charleston, with the thought that I might then be able to get him to consider moving near us, but I got nowhere. Less than two years later, at age seventy-two, he died.

What puzzled me was how someone could have been a successful writer of plays, with five of them on Broadway within a seven-year period, and then so lost his touch that from the late 1930s onward he would write play after play, not one of which would be accepted for performance. I had read of writers who had been "ruined" by having gone to Hollywood and written for the movies, and certainly if one looked at Dan's career, that was what would appear to have happened. Yet the explanation seemed too facile.

In his memoir *The Summing Up,* the English novelist Somerset Maugham, who at one period of his career had been a very successful playwright, examines the abrupt fading of his own vogue in the theater, and remarks that of all art forms, drama is the most volatile and transient. The playwright, Maugham says, must be in complete touch with moods, tastes, and idiom of the day for his work to be successful. The slightest shift in emphasis and topical focus, the slightest adjustment in popular attitudes and nuances, and the dramatist's capacity for conversing with the audience can be destroyed.

If Maugham is correct—and the careers of numerous British and American playwrights would appear to corroborate what he says—then Dan's experience illustrates just that.

I read the typescripts of some of his plays, including not only those written in recent years but those produced in the 1920s and 1930s. Dan's early plays had all been written more or less out of his own observations as a newspaper reporter in the years before and after World War I. His people were lodgers in boardinghouses, newspaper reporters, policemen and detectives, con men, waitresses, working girls, farmers, mainly mid-to-lower-middle class, and described with considerable grim humor and no small amount of sordidness. The plays were melodrama, as the reviews almost always noted, combining ingenious plotting with considerable realism of detail, a keen sense of incongruity, and a good ear for the way that people actually talked.

What I believe may have happened is that when Dan left newspaper work and began writing plays full-time, he lost touch with that everyday milieu. His subsequent experience in Hollywood as a well-paid scriptwriter for Paramount Studios was hardly calculated to renew it. When almost a decade later he went back to writing plays he expected to resume his imaginative access to the people and circumstances from which he had drawn his successful characterizations and settings. But the freshness and authenticity that came of the involvement with everyday life that he had known as a newspaperman was no longer present.

Moreover, theatrical tastes had changed. The hard-boiled, sardonic realism, akin to farce, that had been popular in the 1920s, not only on the stage but in fiction as well, was no longer in demand. The depression of the early 1930s had forced a social consciousness upon the theatergoing public. There was still a place for lower-depths depravity, as evidenced by the longtime popularity of Erskine Caldwell's *Tobacco Road* on the New York stage, but there had to be the sense of economic and social victimization that caused the conditions in which the depravity could function. Cynicism about human nature itself was no longer a sufficient explanation. Meanwhile, a half-century of growing public familiarity with the work of Sigmund Freud meant that there was far more general knowledge, especially in the metropolitan playgoing audience, of the subtleties of human behavior and psychological motivation.

I read a play of Dan's in which the protagonist, a young man, several times went berserk upon hearing the expression "son of a bitch." Ultimately he killed someone and was convicted of murder. Assuming that there was a dimension that I had missed, I asked Dan why the words had so devastating an impact upon the character. Dan's explanation was that he was a clean-minded, good-hearted young man, and the ugliness of the words themselves upset him so that he lost control over his emotions. It was irrational behavior, that was all. Dan's interest was in the dramatic consequences, not in the psychological causes.

On the pre-Freudian stage that might have been sufficient, but not in the 1950s, when the play was written.

Such was the sense I had when I read the plays. Dan had lost the ability to communicate with his potential audience. Their attitudes, assumptions, and demands had changed, while he had not. To cite another example, one of his plays, written probably toward the end of World War II, centered upon a group of veterans who return to civilian life. They fail to secure jobs to replace those they had left to enter the military, and their hopes for love and domestic fulfillment are soon disintegrated. A bleak drama, ending in entire hopelessness, it could scarcely have been less attuned to the mood of the post–World War II years, which were characterized by economic expansion and wide-open professional opportunity, and not only would most returning war veterans find their prewar jobs waiting for them, but numerous other possibilities opening up as well. Without so much as even a temporary lull, the United States went sailing into a postwar boom that continued unabated for several decades. Thus Dan's play went unproduced, for the reason that it bore almost no relevance to the actualities of its time and place.

On my last visit to El Paso we walked across the international boundary on the Rio Grande bridge and into Juárez, Mexico, down the avenue of souvenir stands, silver and leather-goods shops, bars and restaurants, and over to a park, where there was a monument to the Mexican war dead with an eternal flame burning atop it. There were benches in the park, but so spattered with pigeon droppings that we could not sit down until I bought several copies of a newspaper from a vendor to line the seats.

The neighborhood, several blocks away from the tourist shops, was dilapidated, with dirt streets, weeds growing everywhere. The children kicking a soccer ball in one corner of the park were clad in nondescript clothes and obviously from poor families. There was a whitewashed stucco church across the way; someone had chalked a political slogan of some kind beneath the windows. We watched as two old women in black shawls emerged from the doorway and, with the help of canes, hobbled along up the street.

"I don't see how anyone can believe in a God," Dan remarked, "at least in the sense of one who has anything to do with human life as we know it. When you consider the poverty and disease and hunger and squalor all over the world, how could there possibly be a God who is concerned with individual right and wrong?"

Not being versed in theology I made no comment, but the details of the scene, and Dan's remark, engraved themselves on my memory. It seemed to me that the observation was tied in with the compulsion that led him to dwell so often on politics, and to distrust so profoundly the New Deal, the Fair Deal, and the social programs of the Democratic Party. He could not believe the notion that social improvement could be legislated. In his view, which came close to a kind of social Darwinism, it was basic human nature not to want to work for one's livelihood, not to wish to rely upon one's own efforts. All his experience, he thought, showed that only a small proportion of the population was willing or able to supply the hard work, sacrifice, and dedication needed to elevate themselves from depressed circumstances, and these needed no government intervention to do so.

To assure masses of people that they were entitled to a share of the national wealth without having to earn it on their own was in his view to court disaster. When not writing his plays he worried about it constantly. The naïveté and blindness, as he saw it, of the electorate, its vulnerability to fraud, chicanery, and hypocrisy, dismayed and alarmed him. This is why he was so hostile to Communism and anything remotely smacking of socialism.

To understand the intensity of Dan's deeply pessimistic political attitudes, one must take into account not only the conservatism itself, which after all was not exactly an uncommon phenomenon, but the compulsiveness with which he came to insist upon his views, so that he could scarcely write a letter or engage in a conversation without introducing an extended attack on the New Deal, the Fair Deal, the Great

Society, or whatever liberal political stance was currently in fashion. It seems clear that any and all such developments exasperated him almost beyond bearing. Politics had come to symbolize everything that was aberrant about the world.

It was as if he had long since come to doubt the validity of any framework of belief, any system of thought, whether religious, philosophical, social, or political, that purported to explain away the savage incongruities and cruel inequities of the world by ascribing to them a long-range plan or underlying purpose. Highly intelligent, keenly observant, imaginative as he was, he had discovered early on that if he was to extricate himself from poverty and utilize the creative gifts he possessed, he would have to do it for himself. Extenuating circumstances, excuses, alibis would be of no avail. It followed that to attempt to legislate into existence any kind of social amelioration that went beyond opening the way for individual effort was either delusive or self-serving or both.

His plays—those that I read, in any event—all focused on ironies and incongruities. The emphasis, whether for comedy or melodrama, was always upon the discrepancy between intent and result. The characters were typically shown either as pathetically deluded or as calculatingly evil. In the most successful of his plays, *Riddle Me This,* not only the characters in the story but the playgoers themselves are made to appear credulous and easily tricked. We actually witness a man choking his wife to death, and the theater program, "for the benefit of the latecomer," informs the audience, "This is not a mystery play. In the opening scene we saw Dr. Tindal commit the murder and arrange evidence to entrap an innocent man." Yet by the close of the first act we have been led to doubt the evidence of our own eyes and are half-convinced that the murderer could not in fact have committed the crime. There, as in Dan's other plays, the humor is sardonic, mocking; when there is laughter, it is farcical, typically directed at his characters' foibles and weaknesses.

If the urge to write is the urge to identify order and meaning in one's experience through recasting and interpreting it in language, then for Dan the desire to create plays was the desire, and the need, to portray human experience as incongruous and disjunctive. Through seeing it as such he would not then be caught unawares by the mindlessness and savagery of its impact. It should come as no surprise that his favorite work of literature was *Candide;* like Voltaire he felt the need to controvert the shallow philosophical optimism which could hold that all that happened was for the best in the best of all possible worlds. Dan had found it to be otherwise.

In the plays that he wrote during the 1920s and early 1930s, which drew for their subject matter on his experiences among various kinds of people as a newspaperman, he had been able to dramatize the pathos and humor that lay in the chasm between aspiration and actuality—between what his characters sought to do and be and what their actions and hopes brought about.

To write those plays, and to achieve the kind of life in which he could devote himself to the writing of them, he concentrated his thoughts and his energies with singular intensity, drawing upon his extraordinary willpower to make himself focus upon his writing to the exclusion of everything going on around him. He denied himself companionship, creature comforts, diversions, marriage, and a home life.

In so doing, however, he was depriving himself of the one element that could make possible an ongoing deepening of his dramatization of human life as he experienced it—his own continuing imaginative participation in that life. For his successful plays of the 1920s and early 1930s were the product of his youthful involvement in the particulars of everyday life, as observed and mulled over by a perceptive observer whose work as a journalist put him into daily contact with a variety of people and situations. Once he gave up that involvement, he had only the memory of that kind of experience to go on.

Had he been a different kind of writer, this might not have mattered. He might then have been able to enlarge and expand his writing into an exploration, whether philosophical, psychological, or whatever, of his own relationship to those memories. But that was not the way that he saw things. His view of the human condition centered upon the discrepancy between its pretensions and its actualities. It was out of the ironic contradictions between them that he created his plays. To move beyond that into a deepening confrontation with meaning, whether in tragedy or comedy, would have been to grant more cohesiveness, more order and rationality to human existence than he was able or willing to concede.

It is interesting that setting counts for so little in Dan's plays. Except for his Army service in World War I he lived in the South for his first thirty-five years, and throughout his life he was a Southern partisan, yet only one of his Broadway plays takes place there, and this not in Birmingham or Charleston or Atlanta but the farming South, of which he had no personal experience. Even the rural demonology of *Devils* could with equal appropriateness have been set in the Midwest or New England.

His plays not only are thoroughly lacking in autobiographical elements but do not even draw upon the referents of his own personal life. He used to say that all his talent was for dialogue and plotting; he once sent me synopses of a half-dozen situations that he thought would make short stories if I cared to use them. They were centered on ironies, twists of luck, human beings at cross-purposes. Like the action of his plays, they could have taken place just about anywhere.

Writing for the stage is by definition third-person, objective discourse, and it is only the occasional autobiographical play such as Eugene O'Neill's *A Touch of the Poet* that draws with much identifiable directness upon the circumstances of the playwright's own life. In Dan's instance the externality of the dramatic medium would appear to have been uniquely suited to his personality. For although when I was with him he often talked freely and sometimes with startling openness about some of his experiences, I cannot recall his ever saying anything about his emotional life. He kept his feelings to himself.

I sometimes wonder whether the fact that none of his writings ever alluded even indirectly to his youthful circumstance and situation is not an indication of how very intense his emotional engagement with that time and place must have been. Certainly it was not that he was uninterested in the South and in Charleston. On the contrary, he talked about them when I was with him, and he followed the doings of our family closely.

Yet as for what it must have been like not only to be sent away to live in an orphanage, but when at home to feel himself and his family the object of pity, to be a young Jewish boy, slight of stature, in a community that, while known for its cosmopolitan religious life and attitudes, was nevertheless socially very much grouped by class and caste—only very rarely did he ever have anything to say of his feelings about such things, and then usually only indirectly and even unintentionally. When young those feelings had obviously been intense; he had felt his situation keenly.

The very mode of his creativity—total isolation for months at a time, intense concentration on his play to the exclusion of all else— would suggest that an act of the will was involved, as if he were engaged in an effort to displace everyday reality in favor of an imagined world which he could shape to his own purposes.

Several years ago I read an earlier version of this chapter to an audience at the University of South Carolina. The next day I was told that a playwright who was in residence there for a term was very eager to meet with me. My description of Dan's work habits was uncanny, he said; I could equally have been speaking about himself. He too had spent several years in an orphanage. When he wrote he also went into thoroughgoing isolation, seeing no one for weeks and months at a time. The plots and settings of his plays likewise bore no relationship to the events of his own life. It was an interesting similarity.

Why did Dan choose to live by himself in a rented hotel room in western Texas, nearly two thousand miles away from his family and friends? Supposedly it was because the dry atmosphere of the far Southwest eased his nasal condition. Customarily he came home to Charleston for visits every two years or so. He would stay for a couple of weeks, until exposure to the humid seaside air began to make it difficult for him to sleep at night. And I have no doubt that he believed that was all that was involved.

Yet it seems possible to me that in the later years it might well have been that his pride was also a factor. As a youth he had doubtless vowed not ever to return home to live until he had achieved success. To come back to Charleston now would have been to concede that he had failed to do what he had set out to do. Moreover, the thought that others who knew him and his family would feel sorry for him—"There goes poor Dan Rubin, who once used to have his plays produced on Broadway"—would be unbearable.

Whether or not emotions of that nature played a part in Dan's insistence upon living alone and far away from his family, no one can say. If they did, then I feel sure that it was not on any conscious level, because he would never have admitted to himself that such considerations could matter to him. It seems more likely that what happened in Dan's early years constituted so deep a psychological wound that, as I have suggested about the experience at the orphanage, he had screened it from his conscious memory. If this was so, then it may well have been that to be back in Charleston for very long at a time had the effect of evoking associations that, without consciously realizing why, he found oppressive and even threatening.

That of course is speculation. I do know, however, that, as I have suggested, for all his wide reading he had very little knowledge of or insight into what was involved in depth psychology. The workings of the unconscious, the nature of psychosomatic illness, and such matters as that were largely unknown to him.

No one can prescribe or even define what the components of happiness and fulfillment should consist of for someone else. Yet I cannot help but think that Dan *enjoyed* people. He liked good conversation; he was generous, affectionate, considerate; he had a strong sense of family;

he delighted in the company of little children, and was wonderful with them.

I can only conjecture that in the poverty, pain, and dislocation of those terrible early years, he came to believe that to relax his concentration, to indulge himself, to become in any way dependent upon the company of others, was to render himself vulnerable and would constitute a manifestation of weakness. Once confirmed in that assumption, he could never thereafter put it aside. He would not allow himself—except perhaps during that one time in Hollywood when he had considered marrying but had not done so—to admit to a need for others. He must persevere in his solitary way of life. Not to do so would be to give the lie to everything he had set out to achieve. And with his extraordinary willpower—*because* of it—he remained locked into a spartan regimen of self-imposed isolation throughout his life. He was in truth a lonely man, and the more so because he would not concede, on any conscious level, that he was lonely at all.

So he stayed on, by himself, writing his plays. When his eyesight grew so poor that he was told he must give up reading books on a sustained basis, he would listen to music instead. When the cigars that he chain-smoked were ruled out as dangerous to his health, he would give them up then and there. He sat in his room, concentrated upon listening to music; went for walks; glanced through the newspaper.

In the late summer and early fall of 1964, when the conservative wing captured what was to be permanent control of the Republican Party and nominated Senator Barry Goldwater of Arizona to run for president against Lyndon Johnson, Dan's interest in the forthcoming election became so intense that he could not write a letter without devoting the major part of its contents to politics. I had a sabbatical leave from my teaching position, and after several months in Italy we were staying in Florida. I exchanged letters with him at intervals. Not being either a political conservative or a Republican, my failure to agree with his scathing view of the reasons for Goldwater's defeat so angered him that for weeks I heard no more from him. Then he found an occasion to write—to my wife. I replied, as I was meant to do, and we resumed as usual.

At the end of January, 1965, I drove the family up to Chapel Hill, North Carolina, to begin a term as visiting professor. We had been there little more than a week when a telegram arrived from Charleston, informing me that Dan had died of a heart attack. My father was flying down from Richmond for the funeral the following morning. The plane was to stop at Raleigh, and I arranged to join him there.

In the house we had rented in Chapel Hill there was a phonograph and a small collection of classical records. Looking through them I found an old recording of Beethoven's "Romance No. 1 in G Major" for violin and orchestra. The opening was a slow, gravely stated melodic theme on the violin, shyly voiced, as if drawn out from the weight and burden of existence into a hard-won distillation of sweetness.

The music seemed to speak to what my uncle was. Fiercely creative, he had wanted to write plays, and he had done so, teaching himself how to do it, just as he taught himself trigonometry in order to qualify for officers training. He had extricated himself from poverty, had plays on Broadway and movies bearing his name as scriptwriter. When for thirty years the new plays he wrote had gone unacted and unviewed, he never once complained or sought to attribute his failure to get his work produced to any external factor.

However he may be forgotten as a dramatist, certainly by any standard of human worth Daniel Nathan Rubin was no failure. Quite the contrary. He had lived in accordance with his beliefs, and done the very best that he was capable of doing. Throughout his life he was true to himself. When all is said and done, my uncle's life was a thing of bravery and of abiding beauty.

When my father and I arrived in Charleston, we learned that Dan had been stricken while at his hotel, been admitted into a hospital, and had died that night. The body had been shipped from Texas by railroad and was due to arrive in Charleston the next morning. The funeral would be held the day following. He, or rather the thin, small body he had worn, would be buried in the Reform Jewish cemetery on Huguenin Avenue, fronting the salt marsh and the Cooper River.

"I hate to think of Dan riding alone in that cold baggage car," his sister Dora said to me that evening.

"Dora, that's not Dan," I told her; "you know that." And of course she did. But her brother had been very dear to her.

In 1911, when his father died, he had come to that cemetery from Birmingham, the train making a special stop to let him off at Magnolia Crossing. Two years later he went there for his mother's interment. In 1919 the hospital ship bringing him back wounded from France had sailed past the cemetery on its way up the Cooper River to the Navy Yard. In recent years he had been there to bury a brother and a sister-in-law. Now it was Dan's turn. He was coming home to Charleston for good.

5

Strong Cigar

SUNDAY MORNINGS IN THE 1930s my Uncle
Manning would walk along a stone-ballasted embankment leading out
into the Ashley River at the foot of Beaufain Street in Charleston,
choose a seat on the rocks, and begin reading. It was there that my
brother and sister and I would find him.

Across the river, at that point a quarter-mile or more wide, was the
entrance to Elliott Cut, along which the Intracoastal Waterway led
southwestward to the Stono River and then by various creeks, rivers,
and dredged passages behind the Sea Islands to Georgia and Florida.
Not far downstream was the government dock, where the buoy tenders
Cypress and *Mangrove* and an assortment of Coast Guard craft were
based. Upstream, in the tidal flat adjacent to the street extension and
the embankment, was the hulk of an old ferryboat, the *Sappho*,
stripped of its machinery and superstructure and left to disintegrate.
Resting on the bottom, its decaying timbers embedded in the mud, it
had long since ceased to respond to the ebb and flow of the river. A
flimsy walkway led out to it, and a series of loose planks lay across its
rotting deck, permitting access to sailboats and rowboats tied along its
sides.

My uncle enjoyed the outdoors. His face, which particularly in later
years was somewhat more fully fleshed than those of his three brothers, was usually bronzed by the sun. My early memories of him are of
the late 1920s, when we rented summer houses on Sullivans Island and
Manning would come over on his vacation and go fishing every day.

Later, in the 1930s, he took to boating, owning first a rowboat and then two sailboats. After that he gave up the water and began bicycling.

A bachelor, he was born in 1893, two years before my father, and he lived with my Uncle Harry and Aunt Ruth in the large second-floor flat of a sizable house at the corner of Beaufain and Gadsden Streets. Later they built a house on Bennett Street a few blocks away. He was a newspaperman, a reporter for the *Charleston Evening Post,* and then city editor. He had a library of books, and a phonograph with a large collection of classical records. For some years he was a steady reader of western and detective pulp magazines, which he then passed on to my father and to our neighbor Hasell Rivers, but in the early 1930s he changed his reading habits and began subscribing to the *Atlantic Monthly,* the *American Mercury,* and *Scribner's.* It was not a development that my father or Hasell applauded; "Manning's going highbrow on us," Hasell declared.

In his room at Gadsden and Beaufain Streets a wicker bookcase held a number of magazines bearing names such as *Bluebook, Argosy, Munsey's,* and *Dime Detective,* whose pulp paper pages, by then turning brown and brittle with age, contained short stories with his name as author. Some were in collaboration with Octavus Roy Cohen, a boyhood friend who, as noted, had worked with Dan on newspapers in Birmingham. Cohen's parents were friends of our family; as a child in the 1930s I was several times taken to see Mrs. Cohen, who lived on Beaufain Street and had copies of all her son's books. Octy, as he was called, grew up with my uncles and my father. His comic Florian Slappey stories were featured regularly in the *Saturday Evening Post* and collected in book form. On his visits to his mother he always played in the Saturday night poker game. I am told that for all his extraordinary commercial success, both in print and the movies as well, Cohen, who became considerable of a drinker, died broke and owing money to many, including Dan. I always wanted to meet him, but never did.

As for Uncle Manning, he had apparently ceased to write fiction some time back, for all of the magazines bore dates before the 1920s. One day I came across a small volume in his bookcase, bound in dark red cloth and entitled *Profitable Advertising: How to Write and Where to Sell.* by Manning J. Rubin, published by the Hannis-Jordan Company, and likewise dating back to the mid-1910s. I was much impressed, but when I asked him about it he was uncommunicative. I learned later that before he had begun working as a reporter in 1914 he had written advertising for a local department store.

He was a difficult person to converse with under any circumstances, and the older I grew the harder it became. When I began to write fiction I became very interested in family history, and sought to ask him questions about my grandparents and about what life was like for him, my other uncles and aunts, and my father when they were young. But he had nothing to tell. I also tried to question him about the political campaigns that had rocked Charleston during the 1910s and 1920s, which he covered as a newspaper reporter. The mayoral elections of those years had been savagely contested. On one occasion there was a shoot-out when the ballots were being counted, and a reporter for the *Charleston Evening Post,* Sidney Cohen, had been killed.

My father told me that in another local election during the 1910s Octy Cohen's father, Judge Octavus Roy Cohen, Sr., had received threats on his life, and on the eve of the election my father and several others had stood guard at the Judge's residence, armed with pistols. In my father's scrapbooks was a display advertisement featuring a letter from my Uncle Dan, described as a wounded war veteran recovering at an Army hospital in Atlanta, and calling for the defeat of John P. Grace, the Irish American former mayor running for reelection, who was proclaimed as representative of the barbarity and treachery of "the Hun." (Grace had opposed U.S. entry in the war.) Since Dan had not resided in Charleston for almost a decade, the writing and the publication of the letter must surely have been arranged by Manning.

From all I understood, the local population had been divided roughly along class lines, but Manning insisted that no social distinctions or conflicting ideals had been at issue. Both sides, he declared, consisted merely of rival groups of politicians, interested only in getting and holding office.

About politics, as on everything else, Manning had little to say. According to my aunts and my father, however, when younger he had not always been so taciturn. In the 1910s, when my father and my uncles and aunts had lived together following my grandparents' death, he had from all accounts been the liveliest among them, the very soul of wit according to my Aunt Dora. There were tales of the things he had said and done, the jokes he had played. He had been a virtuoso on the harmonica, and had even acted in several plays. By the time I came to know him well, that side of his personality had largely been suppressed. On occasion he could still display considerable humor, but it was sarcastic and often caustic.

Indeed, he had a local reputation for keeping his own counsel. People would encounter him walking along the street and scarcely noticing anyone. There were even theories developed about it. His friend Hasell Rivers was of the opinion that at such times Manning was composing his newspaper stories in his head as he walked. It seems much more likely that my uncle was simply preoccupied with his own thoughts.

Especially in later years he had more or less a standard routine. He got up each morning, ate a sparse breakfast, then departed for his work at the newspaper. He returned home shortly after three o'clock, went at once to his room, and took a nap. Awakening after an hour, he went for a bicycle ride, stopping to visit with groups of small children in the downtown city, who regularly awaited his coming. He usually had some candy for them in his pocket, and he chatted with them, played games, then rode on to the next group. He arrived home in time for his evening meal, which my aunt prepared especially for him and which invariably consisted of boiled chicken, rice, and peas. Then, except for Saturday nights when he played poker, on most evenings he usually retired to his room, where he read and listened to music until time to go to sleep.

He followed this routine week after week, month after month, and year after year, with the exception of two weeks each summer, when he took his vacation. Then he stayed home and read, sailed his boat, or, after he gave up boating and took to bicycling, went on trips of several days' length.

On one occasion he took me with him; we cycled to Walterboro and the next day to St. George, towns within fifty miles of Charleston. Staying in hotels and eating breakfast in restaurants was a new and very heady experience for me. On the final day's journey, a fifty-mile jaunt, we ran into a thunderstorm, got thoroughly drenched, and as we neared the Charleston city limits rode through a puddle which concealed a railroad track crossing the highway. As our tires encountered the groove, first Manning and, a second later, myself went sailing off our bicycles into the water. He made no comment whatever, merely remounting and pedaling off.

There was always a kind of distance between Manning and others, even Hasell Rivers, whom he had known since childhood and who was his closest friend. I never once observed him in easy conversation with another adult. He would listen, and occasionally comment, but seldom volunteer anything of his own or speak of his own feelings and emotions.

I could not imagine Manning participating in any kind of large social group or being part of a civic club or other formal organization. His one group activity was the weekly poker game, usually held at Mr. Rivers's or our house. There were seven or eight regulars, who had been playing together since the 1910s. It was not a high-stakes game. An older cousin of mine who was visiting us and who sat in on it remarked afterward that there were all kinds of wild and ingenious variations difficult for a newcomer to grasp. My father said that Manning was a good player, who usually won. I watched them play occasionally, and his taciturnity seemed perfectly adapted to the activity; he had a natural poker face.

It was only with little children that he seemed completely at ease. Their naturalness and spontaneity intrigued him. He would take part in their games; they were delighted when he played hopscotch and

jackstraws or skipped rope, and sang songs for them. He had a supposed American Indian song, which went something like:

Ah – chick -pan
Oh – polly -oh
E – yi – kee – yi – e – yi – dee - oh
Ru ru - ru
Ru – ru - rururu

Moreover, he could adapt the words to cover every language the world
over. As a child I was very impressed. He also had some phonograph
records of children's songs, including a celebratory epithalamium that
began, "Fiddle-de-dee, fiddle-de-dee, the cow has married the bum-
blebee!" His youthful admirers, comprising several generations of
Charleston families in the neighborhoods where he lived, were legion.
He talked with their parents sometimes, but the adults did not really
interest him.

I once came upon some papers that had belonged to my father in-
dicating, astonishingly to me, that at one time Manning was the grand
master, or whatever the appropriate title, of the local Scottish Rite Masonic Lodge, to which my father also belonged. This had been in the
1910s or early 1920s, when there was considerably more widespread
participation in such activities than in later years. The thought of Manning ever having dressed in Masonic regalia and officiated in rituals
seemed and still seems incredible.

For years he wrote a daily column for the *Evening Post* editorial
page, "While On That Subject," which was bylined with his pen name,
"Strong Cigar." (In actuality he did not smoke cigars but a brand of
cigarettes, "Lord Salisbury," containing a highly aromatic Turkish tobacco; he used a long black cigarette holder, and bought them by the
carton.) "While On That Subject" consisted of a series of comments
and aphorisms on everyday life and political events; they were illustrated with small line drawings, for which he wrote the captions. He
had no firm political position; it was a matter of noting and com-
menting slyly on the absurdities and exaggerations of politicians—but

always national, never local. There was also considerable domestic humor; for an unmarried man he was remarkably observant of the foibles of marriage and domestic life.

Like his brothers, he was self-educated. Uncle Dan once remarked that he did not believe that a college education would have been of any great advantage for himself, but that it would have meant a great deal for Manning, who was by temperament a scholar. Whatever the validity of the idea as it concerned Dan, it was undoubtedly true for Manning. He had the habit of mind of an academic. Under more favorable circumstances, if he had been enabled to continue on to high school and college, it seems quite likely that he would have won scholarships that permitted him to go to graduate school, and might well have become a college teacher.

He was widely read, particularly in the history, literature, and philosophy of classical Greece and Rome. He was familiar with the range of English literature and the classic European novels and plays. In later years his favorite reading was in popular works on archaeology. He also read European history and perhaps American history, but showed no interest whatever in the South or the Confederacy.

He enjoyed travel writing, though he himself never traveled; indeed, the only out-of-state trip I know of that he made other than by necessity was to Richmond for my sister's wedding in 1946. The return leg of that journey was distinguished by a Pullman porter's failure to notify Manning and Dora when the train arrived at the North Charleston station, with the result that the train departed for Savannah with them aboard. Not until the next scheduled stop, at Yemassee, South Carolina, sixty miles farther on, could they debark and be transferred to a returning train. The episode delighted my Uncle Harry, who went about the house singing, "Don't have sense to come in out of the rain, / Don't have sense to get off of the train."

In the mid-1940s the editor of the *Evening Post,* F. O. Emerson, who was one of the Saturday night poker regulars, retired, and Manning was made assistant editor. When I heard the news I was surprised that he did not succeed to the editorship. One of my aunts said that he had been offered the post and had declined it. It would have been quite in character for him to have done so, for so many of the duties that went along with being editor—giving speeches, participating in civic functions, chatting with visiting firemen, conferring with the publisher, and the like—would have been very uncongenial to him. Thereafter, until his own retirement several decades later, he wrote editorials and his daily column.

Nor can I imagine him taking controversial political stands on the issues of the day, particularly on civil rights and racial desegregation, which dominated the news in the 1950s and 1960s. The morning newspaper, the *News and Courier,* was in the thick of the fight, in violently outspoken opposition to racial integration, and although the *Evening Post* was traditionally less combative in its editorial approach, it was expected to and did assume a similar position. Whatever his earlier involvement in local politics may have been, that Manning would have wanted to write such editorials is extremely unlikely. It was not necessarily that he was a dissenter; I do not in fact know what his political views were. But neither would he have been capable of echoing the fiery assertions and extreme statements of South Carolina's political leadership, for he was by nature skeptical and had no use for heady theorizing, inflammatory rhetoric, and frenzied denunciations.

One of the most controversial local figures of the time was a federal judge who, to the consternation and rage of white Charlestonians, delivered a series of rulings that decisively struck down much of the legal paraphernalia on which racial segregation was based. The judge, J. Waties Waring, was a Charlestonian of impeccable Lowcountry ancestry, and before his elevation to the federal bench had been the city's Corporation Counsel. His treason to the cause, as white Charleston saw it, made him the object of obloquy, denunciation, scurrility, and threats of personal violence, the more so because his change of heart was attributed to a Yankee wife he had married after divorcing his Charleston-born bride of many years.

I asked Manning about the judge, whom he had known for years and had worked with during political campaigns in the 1920s and 1930s. His reply was characteristic. He had no belief in the sincerity of the man's newfound concern for racial equality. That the judge, in the process of ruling on federal laws, could have come to a belated realization that his own longtime assumptions and those of his community constituted a profound injustice was in my uncle's opinion quite out of the question. He wasn't the type, he declared; there was not the remotest place for idealism or zeal for equal justice under the law in the judge's makeup. He was just another politician, Manning insisted.

At the same time, Manning had no use for the vocal opposition to the judge or the harassment he underwent. In his view the opponents and denouncers were no better themselves.

Whether Manning was always so pessimistic about human motivation and the efficacy of social change I cannot say. Certainly by the time I grew old enough to query him on such things he had become deeply skeptical. A family story has it that back in 1915, when the city of Charleston was making a recurrent attempt to revive a largely stagnant economy, there was a contest staged for the most appropriate slogan. The winning entry was "Most Convenient Port to Panama," an allusion to the recently completed canal—not exactly a deathless motto. Manning, however, mightily vexed the authorities with an entry that went, "Please Go 'Way and Let Me Sleep."

Having grown up in poverty and known the Great Depression of the 1930s, he was very dubious about economic progress. During the Second World War, Charleston, as a defense center, experienced a decided boom, which did not end when the war was over as had happened in 1919. The Navy Yard and other defense operations continued to thrive; industries established during the war years expanded in size; the multi-thousands of newcomers who had thronged into the area during the war did not depart; the suburbs spread out far beyond the boundaries of the city I had grown up in during the 1920s and 1930s. It was not going to last, Manning told me; all the bustle and optimism and plans for new development would soon collapse. In this he was mistaken. Today the small, somnolent Southern city that he knew has

long since become a metropolis, and its long-tranquil harbor the
second-largest container port on the East Coast.

Though fond of Manning, as a youth I was always rather intimidated
by his laconic manner. That he was basically very shy, and that his taciturnity had its roots in awkwardness, did not then cross my mind.
When in his company I felt that I had something to prove, and that he
was not only older and wiser than I was, but of stronger character,
more spartan, less prone to moral weakness and self-indulgence. Nor
did he hesitate to comment on my activities. On one occasion I was
telling him about the High School of Charleston's football team. "And
how is the Latin team doing?" he asked—a even more pertinent remark
than he knew, for at the time I was engaged in failing my senior year of
Latin.

At the same time I was grateful to him for his generosity. He frequently gave me pocket money, and at Christmas time my mother received a check to buy gifts for us. On one occasion when he bought a
new balloon-tired bicycle for himself, he presented me with his not-
very-old bike, which was far superior to the old narrow-tired Iver Johnson that I owned.

When I reached my mid-teens I grew interested in classical music,
and he allowed me to listen to records on his phonograph when he was
not in. In the 1930s phonographs with drop mechanisms were becoming available, and he began replacing his record collection with albums
with the 78-rpm records arranged so that it was possible to listen to five
or six record sides that, with only brief pauses, played in sequence for
twenty-five minutes and more without having to be turned over. I got
into the habit, on Saturday nights, of going downtown sometimes to
listen to his records and read while he was playing poker. On other
evenings he would often let me know whenever he planned to be out,
so that I could come by if I wished.

I was by then regularly writing news and sports stories for the afternoon newspaper, of which he was city editor, for which I received no
payment. Not once did he ever praise anything I wrote. What I did not

fully recognize, however, was that he was fond of me and very much approved of my interest in journalism and writing as well as in music. I did not understand that his taciturnity, his habit of listening in silence and only occasionally interjecting comments that were more often than not ironical, was not necessarily judgmental, so much as a long-ingrained mannerism that doubtless had its origins in an inability to make small talk.

He was the third son and the fourth-oldest child of my grandparents. What happened in the very early 1900s must have come with a devastating impact on him. He was eight years old at the time, old enough to understand a little of what was going on and to experience some of the humiliation of knowing that others were aware of the family's wretched plight. Of the three brothers who were sent to the Hebrew Orphans' Home, I have the sense that Manning was most affected by the shock of being abruptly uprooted from home. The toughness and fierce pride of Dan was not his; he was not by nature combative. My father was less introspective and self-conscious.

When he returned home he won the gold Bennett Medal for finishing highest in his elementary school class in 1908, then looked on as many of his classmates went on to the High School of Charleston, while he went in search of work. The four or five dollars a week or so that an office boy might expect to earn was desperately needed in a family with three children younger than himself and without a real adult breadwinner—for even after my grandfather recovered somewhat from the illness that immobilized him, he could have sent home only a pittance from the little store he operated in Florence, South Carolina.

What Manning must have feared ever afterward was destitution, the helplessness of being unable to care for oneself. "You should always save one-fourth of your salary," he once told me—which was easier to do if one were a bachelor of abstemious habits and few needs. Yet it was not that he stinted himself. Once the family situation eased in the mid-1910s, he began earning a decent salary. He owned sailboats, and later a series of expensive bicycles. His rooms, in my Uncle Harry's house, were small but tastefully furnished, with Japanese prints on the walls. But always, I feel sure, he kept to that rule of putting aside a fourth of his earnings in savings, and allowed himself to buy luxuries only with what money remained.

Was he ever tempted to marry? There is no way of knowing. His brother Dan did not think so, nor did my mother. My Aunt Essie, who was four years younger, spoke of parties or other social occasions of which he was a part during her girlhood. Photographs taken during the 1910s and 1920s show him as strikingly handsome, with finely chiseled features. He did have female friends; by the time I knew of them they were all married, and he occasionally visited with them and their families. But it seems doubtful that he ever spent much time, even when young, alone in the company of young women.

The solitariness and reserve must indeed have been part of the life of a quiet child of undemanding temperament in a household with parents who were frequently ill. All that then occurred—the orphanage, the hard times, the early deaths of both parents—could only have confirmed those qualities. He was small of stature, with poor eyesight, though in later years he become quite robust. When the war came in 1917 he could not pass the physical examination required for military duty, and I am sure he felt what he would have considered the humiliation involved, the more so because both his next older and his younger brothers were accepted for service.

The abundant wit and humor that from all accounts characterized his behavior within the family during the years when the children were all living together do not, I think, mean that the private nature was not always there. Humor, after all, is based on the perception of incongruity; most humorists are creatures of sadness. Manning's humor, as remarked earlier, tended always to have an ironic quality to it.

He was conscious of being a Jew in a class-conscious community. The family, as I have noted earlier, was affiliated with the "downtown" Reform congregation, among whose members there was sometimes considerable self-consciousness about their social position vis-à-vis the "uptown" Orthodox Jews. But Manning's skepticism and self-mockery would have seen through this as well, and have identified such pretension for the absurdity that it was.

Many years later, in 1961, I published a novel in which one of the themes I sought to portray was just that snobbishness, which had been injected into my consciousness during my own childhood. Because I was writing fiction I had to dramatize my youthful protagonist's inherited social attitudes, in order then to allow him to commence the lengthy process of divesting himself of them—a process that would be part of a larger distancing from the community. From my own experience I knew how long it had taken to accomplish that. I thought it important to show that the elements that would culminate in my protagonist's separation were seemingly, at his age, only of minor importance—as they had been, on any conscious level at least, for myself at the age of twelve. My model was the way in which at the conclusion of *Adventures of Tom Sawyer,* which as a child and youth I read over and over, it is clear to the adult reader that Tom is growing away from the town of St. Petersburg, but that Tom does not realize it.

So far as Manning was concerned, I did too good a job of it, for he censured me for exhibiting anti-Semitism. I was disappointed, for while I knew that my aunts, despite all their affection for me, would find it difficult to accept the artistic necessity of portraying youthful bigotry to show its insidiousness—they would prefer that the subject be eschewed entirely*—I had assumed that Manning would understand what I was trying to do. And he might well have been able to do so, had it been somebody else's novel; but not in mine. For that was too close to home. By contrast, my Uncle Dan got the point at once.

As noted, Manning lived with my Uncle Harry and Aunt Ruth. When Harry died, in the late 1950s, Manning and Ruth moved to a double

*My Aunt Ruth reported that at her sewing circle, made up of various Jewish matrons, someone had objected to what I had written, to which another member had replied, "Well, that's the way it used to be in Charleston, wasn't it?"

apartment. Ruth died in 1963, and thereafter he lived by himself. A cook came in to prepare a simple meal for him each evening. "I eat only to live," he told me once. When I visited Charleston I always stopped in to see him. We would talk a little, but with as much difficulty as ever.

In the early 1960s he suffered an attack of angina pectoris and was hospitalized for several weeks. He detested every minute of it. I had some books on archaeology and ancient history around the house, and I sent them to him. He enjoyed reading them, and wrote me to that effect. The next time I saw him, after he was back home and about, he told me that he wanted nothing more to do with hospitals.

After his death in 1967 his friend Hasell Rivers, who lived in the same apartment house, wrote my father that Manning had remarked a few days earlier that the angina was causing trouble once again, and that he was not going to take the nitroglycerin tablets that had been given him for use in future attacks. Had he done so he could very likely have lived a few years more, but he had decided that it was not worth the price of the hospitalization and enfeeblement.

I asked him once why he had ceased to write fiction. He replied only that "I lost interest in it." Yet sometime in the late 1940s, while in his rooms one evening listening to phonograph records, I saw a recently typed short story with his name on it. The title page indicated that it was written for submission to a competition conducted by *Ellery Queen's Mystery Magazine.*

Most of the pulp short stories that he published were the product of the early 1910s. They were intricately plotted, as was appropriate for the magazines that published them. His fiction writing appears to have tailed off considerably after he became a reporter for the *Charleston Evening Post.* Obviously a daily regimen of writing for a newspaper inhibits one's efforts to write on one's own. Yet there are working journalists who do manage to write plays, stories, magazine articles, and books, even novels.

A more likely explanation, it seems to me, lies in the fiction he did publish. He wrote about detectives, and policemen who solved crimes, and about ingenious domestic situations. None of his stories that I have seen could have been drawn from his own experience. They were essentially exercises in plotting and did not involve an effort to explore emotional depth and complexity.

His own choice of reading matter was never confined to pulp fiction, which in any event he stopped reading in the early 1930s. The books in his library, dating from the 1910s and 1920s onward, included literary and philosophical classics, many of them in the old Boni and Liveright Modern Library editions, and he also made regular use of the Charleston Library Society collection. Ancient history and, later, prehistory were his favorite fare. He was not of course trained in the classical languages or archaeology, and his interest in the latter was of a nonspecialized nature.

I believe that Manning stopped writing fiction because, although he had certainly read the English and European classic novelists, he thought of it almost entirely as diversionary reading. As for writing nonfiction, he did not possess the professional knowledge to write about the subject matter he was most interested in—ancient history, the Greek and Roman philosophers and poets, archaeology. This is what his brother Dan meant when he said that Manning would have benefitted greatly from a college education. His interests and concerns were essentially scholarly—but without the training to work professionally in the subjects that intrigued him. He remained a newspaper journalist, and a very good one indeed. Clearly he could have moved on to larger, metropolitan newspapers, but he chose to remain in Charleston.

After his retirement from the *Evening Post* he wrote what proved to be a very popular series of feature articles on a fiercely contested election for mayor of Charleston in 1923 between the incumbent John P. Grace and Thomas P. Stoney. It was an unusual election in that it was waged along lines of class by two skilled and articulate politicians. I had become interested in the campaign, and Manning saved a set of carbon copies of his articles for me. They consisted entirely of description and were written without any attempt at setting either the campaign or the protagonists within what was obviously the social, or for that matter political, context.

The series, in short, was consistent with the position he had taken when I once questioned him about the John P. Grace–era elections, which was that no real ideology or social division was involved, but solely a matter of officeholding. Yet though neutral as a reporter, Manning had been deeply engaged. He had been closely associated with Thomas P. Stoney and his supporters, and had helped with strategy and written campaign material, though he neither sought to profit from it nor would accept any largesse. Stoney's successor as mayor, Burnet R. Maybank, who later became governor and U.S. senator from South Carolina, esteemed Manning highly, as did various other members of the local political establishment.

It is as if he drew a strict line of demarcation between his everyday experience and any thoughts he may have had about the larger social, political, or philosophical implications—more than that, as if he refused to acknowledge that such implications existed.

During the Second World War, I was in Charleston on leave from Fort Benning, Georgia, and he gave me a book by W. Macneile Dixon, *The Human Situation,* which impressed me a great deal. It was a non-theological but idealistic work, with the chapters prefaced by passages from Vaughan, Traherne, and the Cambridge Platonists, none of whose writings I had yet encountered. Ultimate meanings, however, were one thing, and the events and particularities of his life another, and he had, probably early on, erected a protective barrier designed to keep them separate in his mind, much like the Stoic philosophers whose writings he read.

Was there much happiness in his life? Satisfaction, I should say, rather than outright happiness: principally, it seems to me, in his dealings with little children, who loved him, looked up to him, and waited his advent each evening. I do not mean by this that he was unhappy, so much as that from his childhood onward he had learned so to moderate and even repress his expectations that he had severely limited the occasions for outright joy. Certainly in his adult life he could not have known what it was to share, fully and totally, an emotional experience with someone else.

From my childhood on I knew him, admired him, thought about him, tried to fathom what made him as he was. He remains an enigma, a mystery. His brothers I think I can understand, complex personalities though they were—even Dan. The wellsprings of their conduct seem comprehensible to me. But not Manning's.

Was there a mystery at all? I ask myself that sometimes. Is it rather that he was shy, basically literal-minded, and in actuality fairly straightforward in his thoughts? Does the apparent enigma derive from a child's observations of an adult, and the attribution, to a noncommunicative, somewhat oblique personality, of unfathomed depths that may not have been present at all? For there is always the temptation to take silence as golden, and to assume it is the outward sign of inward wisdom. Was Manning merely *ironic*—given to noting contradiction and expressing it, without any particular wish to explore beyond what was incongruous?

I feel certain that there *was* considerably more than was present on the surface, but I do not know; it comes down finally to that. His next-older brother, Dan, with whom he was closest, and I used to talk about him sometimes. On one occasion Dan expressed doubt that Manning had ever been importantly involved with a woman. Whether Dan thought that his brother's solitary ways were the product of timidity, or reserve, or both, he did not say. I have noted that he believed Manning's cast of mind was essentially scholarly and reflective rather then creative. (Dan's was certainly creative enough.)

Manning *knew* things; there is no doubt of that. As I have said, he possessed a wide knowledge of Roman and Greek history, and of ancient civilization. He also knew the facts and sources of local civic and political life, as befitted a newspaper editor. Once, in the course of writing a novel, I wanted to obtain some information about a murder that happened in the mid-1930s, when I was a youth. Manning at once provided the name of the victim, a trolley car motorman whose wife had

shot him to death and then took her own life, and guided me to the appropriate file in the newspaper library.

Since he had been city editor of the *Evening Post* at the time when
the killing took place, it is not surprising that he was able to remember
it a quarter-century later. Yet something about the way that he immediately identified it stuck in my mind. I cannot put my finger precisely
on what it was, but I had the feeling that here was a man who, whatever
his off-duty musings, his reading, his personal interests, was fully im-
mersed in the work he had been doing for what then had been almost
forty years. He was *of* it; it was the conscious reality, the dominating
concern, of his life. In this, I believe, he differed from Dan, and from
me as well. We were essentially observers; Manning was a participant.

Not that any such distinctions are absolute, to be sure, or that we
too could not become engrossed in the details of our immediate experience, too. But for better or worse—and the relative worthiness of the
two approaches is not at issue—there was a kind of distance, or remove, between our ways of looking at everyday reality and our place
within it on the one hand, and our daily engagement with that reality
on the other, that did not work in quite the same way for Manning.

Yet in another, different sense the distancing was there for him, and
if anything even more abidingly. It was not a separation between himself and his work, or himself and his reading or his other leisure-hour
pursuits, but between him and the world, including everyone and
everything of and in it. My error, perhaps, had been to think of it in
terms that were philosophical or social in nature. It was other, and
more, than that: psychological in makeup and far more thoroughgoing.
In a deeper, more complete, and perhaps more ultimate way than anyone else I have ever known, he was *alone*—more so even than Dan, for
whom isolation was a deliberately willed condition.

Whether through temperament or childhood circumstance—probably both—there was a solitude in Manning, a reserve, that found no
outlet into the world except perhaps through the music he loved so
much to listen to—always alone, on the phonograph, never in public
at concerts. It was very basic and all-encompassing. So early had it

descended upon him, and so complete were its manifestations, that there was neither urgency nor compulsion about it. It was too comprehensive for urgency, and too thoroughgoing and constant to be compulsive. Only with little children could its rigor, however guardedly, be relaxed, and he could be gentle and direct and without sarcasm or wariness.

His needs, his desires were, finally, very simple. On one visit I was surprised to find certain books and objects out on his table and at his bedside: an anthology of sentimental poems; a book of old songs; an album of photographs, the emulsion long since shaded into sepia, of himself, his brothers and sisters and their friends during the 1910s and early 1920s. All his life he wore on his keychain the gold medal he had been awarded after his seventh and final year of Bennett School. I wonder whether, when he heard those old songs being sung on the radio or television, he sang along with the music:

> *Tell me the tales that to me were so dear,*
> *Long, long ago, long, long ago.*
> *Sing me the songs I delighted to hear*
> *Long, long ago, long ago.*

He died as he had lived, alone, quietly, in his sleep. It was two days before his body was discovered.

Hyman L. and Fannie Sanders Rubin, 1892 or 1893, with three oldest children, *left to right,* Dan, Harry, and Dora

Dan, *seated,* Manning, *left,* and Louis. This photo was apparently taken not long after their admission to the Atlanta Hebrew Orphans' Home in 1902. Note the shaved heads.

Hyman and three daughters, *left to right,* Esther, Dora, and Ruthie, taken about 1907–1908

Dora in 1912

Hyman and Louis, probably 1910

Manning about 1910

Manning, as news reporter, aboard interned German freighter *Liebenfels* with captain and officer, Charleston harbor, 1914–1916

Dan in Army uniform, 1917

Louis in Marine uniform, Camp Paoli, Pa., 1918

Louis and Jeanette Weinstein Rubin, 1921–1922

Charleston Electrical Merchants Association, September 1923.
Louis, chairman, is seated, center.

Photo by J. F. Short

Manning, about 1940

Dan at Carmel, Calif., 1930s

Harry and Ruth Ensel Rubin, 1930s

Ruthie in Columbia, S.C., 1940s

Dora arriving in Richmond for a visit to the escalators,
about 1960

Dora, Essie, and Ruthie, 1970s

6

The Weatherman

WHEN IN 1955 I PUBLISHED my first book, a friend telephoned my father to offer congratulations. Unlike his three brothers my father was not much on reading, and he tended to get his literary references confused. He had in mind the fables of the ugly duckling and the black sheep, but the distinction was not quite clear in his mind. "Yes," he agreed, "it's the story of the black duck!"

He was the youngest son, and as with the others his formal education ended with the seventh grade, after which he went to work. Highly intelligent, imaginative, he was also endowed with abundant energy as well as considerable persistence. His bent was practical and, though untrained, implicitly scientific. A self-made man if ever there was, he ended up having not one but two quite separate careers. When he died, at age seventy-five, the television stations in Richmond, Virginia, where he lived for the latter decades of his life, ran documentaries about him. If only he could have seen them! For he loved the limelight.

He was born in Charleston, May 31, 1895. When he and two of his brothers were sent off to live at the Hebrew Orphans' Home in Atlanta he was seven years old. He stayed there for three years, returned home, graduated from Bennett Elementary School in 1909, and found a job as an office boy with a wholesale paper company and then a hardware dealer, I. M. Pearlstine Co. For many years a red wagon wheel hung over the East Bay Street sidewalk above the Pearlstine storefront; my father had installed it.

He became interested in the then-newfangled use of electricity, and by the time he was fifteen he had begun doing repair and installation work. A business card printed in 1910 read:

———— TAKE NOTICE ————
LOUIS D. RUBIN
ELECTRICIAN

———

26 Pitt Street — Charleston, S.C.
Electric Lights and Bells Installed
And Repaired
Telephone 2673-J   All Work Guaranteed

On the back were various useful telephone numbers, so that the card would be kept for reference.

Within a couple of years he was no longer working out of the family home and had rented a counter in Strohecker's Hardware Store on King Street, where he displayed electric lamps, fans, and other consumer goods. By 1916—he was twenty-one—he had a retail store and a contracting business of his own, with electricians and sales clerks in his employ.

These doings did not go unremarked. There are newspaper items on every stage of his career thereafter. As the fifth child and fourth son in the family, he was eager for attention, public and private both. I have the sense that the experience of being sent to the orphanage did not cause him to turn inward, as happened with his brothers Dan and Manning, but instead intensified his ambition to make something visible of himself.

As an adult, at about five feet seven inches he was the tallest of the brothers, though not the most athletic. He was grateful to the orphanage and those who were in charge; throughout his life, whenever there was occasion for memorializing or honoring someone, he sent a gift to the Hebrew Orphans' Home. But more than most people, he existed for the present and the future. While he maintained elaborate scrapbooks displaying his accomplishments, he was never content with his laurels; he was constantly planning new feats. Throughout his life he had to be doing something. Although on occasion this could cause problems, generally it was a valuable trait to have.

After the United States entered World War I he received a warrant as a technical sergeant in the Marine Corps and turned his business over to an aide. He trained in a signal battalion at Paoli, Pennsylvania, and the Philadelphia Naval Station, but the war ended before he was sent overseas. Like many thousands of others he was hospitalized with influenza during the epidemic of 1918, but he recovered and was discharged from the Marines in the spring of 1919. During my childhood his uniform was kept in our attic, and by the time I was fifteen it fitted me nicely. He had said he wanted to be buried in it, but later he must have changed his mind, because by the time of his death in 1970 it had disappeared.

After the war his electrical business moved into high gear. He was greatly interested in the new contrivance of commercial radio, and news stories appeared about the distant stations he was able to raise on his receiving equipment. As a merchant his forte was creating interesting show windows displaying new electric appliances. He spent much time planning and developing these, and made a point of entering contests, in which his imagination and ingenuity won him numerous prizes from electrical publications and merchandising associations, among them an automobile, a chest of silverware, and an elaborate radio receiving set in a large standing cabinet. (The radio was quickly outmoded; I still have the cabinet.) He was active in business groups, president of the Retail Merchants Association, very much on the civic scene and in the news. His electrical-construction company's sign appeared on numerous building projects.

In 1927 his company moved into new quarters, previously a movie theater, with a formidable marquee above the broad show window and entrance. It was an appropriate match: in business and in showmanship he was decidedly an impresario. The afternoon newspaper contained an eight-page advertising supplement highlighting the new store, with congratulatory ads from other merchants. The electrical trade magazines featured the store, with photograph displays; in one of them he was proclaimed the nation's leading retail electric dealer, in another the "Dixie Dynamo."

Meanwhile in 1921 he had married Jeanette Weinstein, from Richmond, and by 1927 there were two sons and a daughter. I was the oldest, followed by my sister, Joan Claire, and my brother, Edwin Manning. My mother was the daughter of an Austrian-born jeweler. Affectionate, even-tempered and steady of purpose, without intellectual interests, she was the ideal wife for my father. She kept him anchored in reality when his ideas threatened to take off into the empyrean, while his range of activities and concerns held her interest after her own rather staid background.

The late 1920s were the good years. His electrical construction business began to involve industrial contracts in nearby cities as well as Charleston. His retail store flourished; for the Christmas seasons he set up in his show window an elaborate operating display of electric trains, which drew large crowds. He developed and patented a heavy, adjustable floodlamp on rollers, designed for use in automobile-repair shops. There were high hopes for it, but ultimately it appears not to have been a success, because the only example remained in our basement throughout the 1930s.

He was active in the Rotary Club and the American Legion. Several times a week he played golf; I still own a special long-shafted "septem jigger" club he bought for making approach putts, as well as a loving cup he won in a local tournament, I assume in a fairly lowly flight, for he told me he had never broken 90 for eighteen holes. My mother also took up golf, playing with friends. I recall once, as a six- or seven-year-old, asking at dinnertime, "Daddy, why don't you and mother play golf together?" and receiving a somewhat less than clear-cut explanation.

In the spring of 1931, he returned from playing golf with a head cold which produced a severe earache. Wrongly diagnosed as mastoiditis and operated on, it developed into a dangerous brain abscess. At a

hospital in Richmond he underwent three operations and was not expected to live, but he eventually recovered, although for some months
afterward his left side was paralyzed. His illness came as the nation was
sliding into the great economic depression, and his business, left in the
hands of a none-too-scrupulous assistant, did not survive.

In the summer of 1932, at the age of thirty-seven, he returned to
Charleston from Richmond, his head heavily bandaged, unable to go
back to work, forced to look on as the electric company he had built
out of nothing went bankrupt, and with a wife and three small children
dependent upon him.

In effect he had seemingly replicated his own father's career, as he
must have realized. However, the memory of the ordeal of three little
boys being uprooted from their home and sent away to an orphanage
had prompted him, once he married and became a father, to purchase
disability coverage. There was also insurance for disability from his
World War I service in the Marine Corps. Thus his family was ade-
quately provided for, and if not well off, certainly reasonably comfortable.

The impact on his morale was, however, devastating. He had always
been extroverted, expansive, and optimistic. On the evening before surgery for the most perilous of his brain abscesses, when he had been all
but given up for lost, he bet the rabbi who had come to pray with him
that within a couple of months' time he would be shooting a game of
craps with him. He won the bet. Decades later, he told me, he was waiting for a bus in Richmond when a motorist stopped to offer him a ride.
After he got in the car the motorist stared at him. "My god, I thought
you'd died back in 1931!" he declared. It seems the man had been a pa-
tient in the adjacent hospital room.

But it was no longer possible for my father to assume that, if only
he worked hard enough and long enough, he would be able to do anything, achieve any goal that he set for himself. He was compelled to
look inward, to confront his limitations and a sharply diminished future prospect.

The enforced idleness, the need to withdraw from the various civic activities in which he had been involved, the necessity for the first time since his early years to restrict his spending, and perhaps the absence of any occasion for public notice—these were very disturbing. No longer were there the Rotary Club and Retail Merchants sessions, although he did continue to attend the American Legion Post No. 10 meetings. He sought to take up reading, notably books on popular science, but he lacked the patience to do so for very long at a time. He even tried writing short stories, which since he had no literary skills whatever were appallingly bad.

We were living downtown in a flat just below Broad Street, having moved from a much larger rented house on Hampton Park Terrace, and on one occasion my mother woke up late at night to find him gone from his bed and the house. She telephoned my local aunts and uncles, and a search began for him. He was found several blocks away on Murray Boulevard, standing at the railing and staring at the waters of the Ashley River below. This episode was kept from us at the time, but when I look back I can see that as a ten- and eleven-year-old I sensed my father's deep unhappiness.

It was in order to provide him with an outlet for his reviving energy that, early in 1935, we built a new house at the foot of Sans Souci Street in the northwest edge of the city. As a stimulus to the depression-ridden economy the Roosevelt administration had developed a program whereby low-interest mortgages for residential construction were guaranteed by the federal government. My father's loan application was approved. The building contractor, C. W. Blanchard, liked to tell how, after the agreement was signed, my father appeared in his office with an accordion-type letter correspondence file for him. "Before we're done," he warned Blanchard, "I'm going to fill this up."

By then he had made a recovery, although his left side remained somewhat weak. He was also subject to what were called "nervous spells," whose advent he always carefully recorded. At that period there was little medical understanding of such things in places such as Charleston, but it seems likely that the origins of the "nervous spells" were less physiological than psychological.

During those years there were references to "if I go back into business," and it may well have been that by the middle 1930s, from the
standpoint of his physical health he could have done so. There exists a
letter offering him a position with the South Carolina Power Company.
A considerable gamble would have been involved, for by accepting employment he would have voided his disability insurance. If he then
proved unable to "stand the strain," as it was expressed, his family's
well-being would be jeopardized. He did not accept the offer. In any
event, it is scarcely surprising that the state of his health was a constant
preoccupation, constituting as it did an explanation for his "failure"—
there were times when he probably viewed it as such—to resume a
business career.

The new house, located on a bluff overlooking the Ashley River and
marsh in what was then a mile-long, half-mile-wide area of fields,
woods, and thickets, was built high off the ground on brick pillars, in
the center of a rectangular tract. As a device to occupy my father's attention, it succeeded very well indeed. For the next seven years, most of
his conscious attention and whatever money was available went into it.

He became an passionate gardener, working at it each morning and,
after a nap, late afternoon. The portion of the property along Sans
Souci Street was given over to the cultivation of roses. He grew them in
great profusion, with numerous varieties planted along both sides of a
horseshoe driveway, in clusters here and there, and entwined in arbors.
Within a few years the rose garden began attracting attention, and he
saw to it that when the blooming was at its height, word of it appeared
in the newspaper, so that on Sunday afternoons people drove down to
the foot of the street to observe the display.

He established relationships with the county agricultural agent and
sought his counsel in purchasing and transplanting trees and shrubs.
A sizable pecan tree was installed next to our house. When the agent
told him that at least a year would have to go by before it began to bear,
he secured a leafy branch with several pecans on it, mounted a ladder,
wired it well up in the tree, then called the agent to report the new

development. Only upon close inspection by the agent, who hurried over to see the seeming miracle, did the hoax become evident.

He wanted shade trees as rapidly as possible. Reading horticultural catalogs and Department of Agriculture bulletins, he learned of a variety of North China elm that developed height and branches with remarkable swiftness, and he ordered several, which quickly made themselves at home and flourished. When in 1938 a tornado roared through downtown Charleston, uprooting and destroying all the shade trees in Washington Park, he lost no time in informing the city authorities about his trees, and a photograph duly appeared in the newspaper, showing the director of parks inspecting his North China elms.

The Charleston area was considered too northerly for growing oranges, but he saw this as a challenge. He installed a temple orange tree, tended it carefully, and by the late 1930s it was bearing an abundance of large golden oranges. A photograph of this too appeared in the newspaper.

By the early 1940s what had been a bare lot with a newly built dwelling on it had become an elaborate garden with flower beds, trellises, a wide lawn, and trees. The house now had an enclosed basement. A portion of the side porch was screened in, making it possible on summer nights to sit outside in defiance of mosquitoes. In one corner of the yard a stone grill was in place for broiling hot dogs and hamburgers.

Meanwhile the open areas to the north, east, and south, which when we first moved in were fields, thickets, and creeks, were now built up, criss-crossed with streets and lined with homes. My father was named head of a commission to explore the paving of the streets, and before we moved away not only Sans Souci Street but other thoroughfares in the northwestern corner of town were being paved.

He continued to take part in the doings of the American Legion post. As chairman of the properties committee, when the post moved its headquarters in the late 1930s he discovered, packed in boxes in the basement armory, the discarded dress uniforms of a once-active

National Guard unit which had been disbanded twenty years earlier.

He did not rest until a use could be found for the uniforms. He arranged to donate them to Jenkins Orphanage, and thereafter on Saturday mornings on King and Broad Streets, at festive events, at the arrivals of trains and passenger liners, and on other appropriate occasions, a band of youthful Afro-American musicians made their appearance, clad in the cut-down Confederate-gray uniforms of the Charleston Light Dragoons, with horns and reeds tootling away and drums rattling, while several of the smallest members moved about the crowds passing the hat.

Not always did his compulsiveness have such beneficent results. He grew irked when our longtime cook Florence's teenage son William preferred to do yard work for our neighbor Hasell Rivers, who was away at his real estate business throughout the day, rather than for my father, who was on hand to oversee William's every activity. Florence either could not or would not—probably both—insist that William alter his preferences. My father was unable to accept this, and the upshot was that both Florence's hours of duty and her wages were reduced, whereupon Florence quit her job. Thereafter my mother was without satisfactory help, and the added burden, together with the cumulative strain of my father's severe illness and the events of recent years, triggered a nervous collapse and the need for her to go off to Richmond for some weeks to recuperate.

In 1942 my parents decided to sell the house and move to Richmond, where my mother's elderly father lived. The reasons for the move were largely financial. My father's income remained fixed, while the requirements of a household with three teenage children—I was by then a sophomore at the College of Charleston—were steadily intensifying. Medicines and visits to physicians were expensive; in Richmond two of my mother's brothers were physicians. The physical demands of tending the garden had also become more onerous. I believe, too, that the novelty of creating a garden out of an empty field had begun to pall, now that the pleasure of planning, selecting shrubs, and transplanting them had become principally a matter of pruning and tending.

In Richmond my parents purchased a home with only a small front lawn and backyard, and no garden to tend. When my grandfather, who had come to live with us, died in the fall of 1943, my mother was part inheritor of his jewelry store, and my father, for want of anything else to do, began riding the streetcar downtown each day and handling the bookkeeping. I was in the Army by then and do not know what else he found to keep himself occupied. Living in a much larger city, where he was unknown and had few friends, none of them on the local newspapers, must have been difficult.

He did have one big moment. Our house was heated by a coal furnace. One day he noticed a pipe, its end capped, which protruded from the brick wall of the cellar and seemed to lead underneath the side porch, for what purpose he did not know. So he got a shovel and began digging in the area alongside the porch. He uncovered what looked to be the side of a large metal cylinder, and further excavation revealed the presence of a tank filled with 264 gallons of heating oil. Apparently, when the previous owner of the house had replaced an oil furnace with the present coal furnace, the fuel tank had been left in place. Sealed off in an airtight tank, the heating oil was still quite usable. This was during the war, when the supply of fuel oil for household use was severely rationed. Needless to say, a story appeared on it in the newspaper. It was picked up by a cartoonist, and a drawing of my father and the tank was widely circulated.

This kind of constitutional unwillingness to let things go uninvestigated was characteristic. One evening after the war was over, my sister was entertaining her fiancé in our basement recreation room. About 10 P.M. my father made his customary trip downstairs to check the condition of the furnace before retiring. As always he descended the cellar steps with his glance carefully averted from where my sister and the boyfriend were installed on a sofa listening to the radio.

This time, however, he noticed an odd-looking place in the brick-work across the way and went over to investigate. There were termites coming through the mortar.

He got the vacuum cleaner, hooked it up, and began drawing them out of the wall. The dust bag was soon filled with a mass of wriggling white bugs. He displayed them to my sister and her boyfriend, then took the bag upstairs to show my mother and myself. By then more ter-mites had arrived in the brickwork, and he extracted these as well, after which he called it quits for that evening.

In the morning there was a new supply of termites. He began tele-phoning pest control companies and found one that would do the ex-terminating the way he wanted it done. However, there would be a two-day wait before the work could be commenced, and to ask my fa-ther to stand by idly while termites were occupying the foundations of his house was to demand the impossible. From time to time he vacu-umed out another load of termites. Additional termites materialized in replacement of those removed, and he vacuumed out those. And so on. For two days there was the recurring sound of a vacuum cleaner work-ing away in the basement.

When finally the exterminator showed up to begin work, my father showed him the place in the brickwork where the termites had been appearing and told him what he had been doing. "I hate to tell you this, Mr. Rubin," the exterminator announced after surveying the situation, "but you been drawing in termites from all over this side of Rich-mond!" So the story goes.

Except perhaps in the years just before we built the new house on Sans Souci Street, when he tried to interest himself in works of popular sci-ence, I cannot recall my father ever reading a book solely for the pleas-ure of it. Sometime in the 1920s he purchased a set of the *Harvard Classics,* "Dr. Eliot's Five-Foot Shelf of Books," but that he actually read any of them, or any of the elaborately printed *Collected Works of Elbert Hubbard,* the "Sage of East Aurora," I very much doubt. His favorite book was a hefty volume entitled the *Home Medical Encyclopedia,* which he scanned over and over again in search of diagnoses for assorted maladies. He once assured me that with it he could himself diagnose and treat any illness.

A taste that he did share with several of his brothers, and with myself, was for classical music. Each evening at dinnertime, in the years before the advent of long-playing records, he would place a half-dozen 78-rpm disks on his phonograph. He especially liked overtures, and he had several albums of them, which however were not designed for a phonograph with a drop mechanism but meant to be played separately, first one side and then the other. To do that, however, required getting up every four minutes to change them, so instead he would play all the front sides, then all the versos. For a time there would be one orchestral buildup after another, each halted while only partway through. Then would come a period of musical pandemonium, with one crashing climax following another, until the last record had dropped down onto the turntable and been played.

During the later war years, my sister several times invited young men she had met who were stationed at Fort Lee, not far from Richmond, to have Sunday dinner with the family. On one such occasion the guest inadvertently spilled some gravy. "Oh, don't worry about that!" my father assured the young man, who was obviously embarrassed. "It happens all the time!" To prove his point he ladled additional gravy onto the tablecloth.

It was during those years, the late 1940s and early 1950s, that he embarked on the project that was to dominate the later part of his life. He had always been interested in the weather, and in the 1920s bought and thereafter regularly consulted a "Cyclo-stormograph," a recording barometer which registered barometric pressure on a chart affixed to a slowly revolving cylinder, so that a week's rise and fall was indicated by a continuous line. He was also aware of the relationship between the progression of cloud formations, the direction of the wind, and changes in the weather. Later, in interviews, he would declare that it was while he had been lying on his back for weeks at a time during his hospitalization for brain abscesses, with nothing else to do but watch the clouds overhead through the window, that he had become interested in weather prediction.

That weather changes were heralded by the procession of clouds and altered wind direction had of course long since been known, but what he did was to perceive that by comparing pictures of successive cloud formations with the clouds in view overhead, it was possible for someone unschooled in meteorology to forecast local weather changes. All that was necessary was to match up the clouds and to determine which way the wind was blowing. To further his objective he purchased and installed an electrical device that, registering the movements of a vane mounted atop the roof of our house, flashed the direction of the wind and the steadiness with which it was blowing onto a dial displayed in the living room. The blinking light, veering as the wind shifted, fascinated my mother, who could watch it for hours.

He decided to assemble a booklet in which the various cloud formations would be illustrated, with a legend underneath each picture giving the requisite information for predicting what the forthcoming weather would be. To do this, he began combing through all the magazines he could find, looking for color photographs of the sky. A good deal of searching was involved, but eventually he located the cloud patterns he wanted, often as the background in advertisements. From these he cut out a series of rectangles, pasted them in a vest-pocket-sized leaflet of twelve pages, wrote captions for them, and prefaced them with a brief statement explaining his method. With this he approached a local printer, MacLean Whittet, who recognized its potential and expressed interest in working with him.

Before that happened, however, he came close to selling his booklet for next to nothing. He had written to an advertising concern in Baltimore about it, and not long afterward a representative of the firm came to see him. He had in his pocket a check for $300, he said, in exchange for the full rights to the project.

My father was tempted. He had no sure idea of its value, twenty years had gone by since he had last had business dealings, and $300 was in 1950 a sizable amount of money. Fortunately he turned down the offer.

The printer had color separations made and produced a sample booklet, entitled *How to Forecast the Weather,* with the back cover left blank for an advertisement. My father began writing to various corporations, offering the booklet for sale. One of the first big purchases came in 1951, to an insurance company, Mutual of New York, which had built a skyscraper in downtown Manhattan with an illuminated tower that turned various colors in accordance with the weather forecast. A hundred thousand copies of the booklet, with information about the tower and the company on the back, were distributed as a promotional giveaway. Thereafter Mutual of New York ordered additional copies every few years. Other companies large and small likewise purchased quantities of the book. During the next two decades, up to his death in 1970, several million copies of *How to Forecast the Weather* were distributed.

He was dissatisfied with the quality of the illustrations, however, and since there was no good source for color cloud photographs, he began taking his own. He amassed a collection of photos and slides that not only answered his own needs but began to be ordered by the U.S. Department of Commerce and by textbook and encyclopedia publishers. In the late 1950s he developed a wall chart, which also found widespread use. Government aviation and agricultural bureaus and businesses with outdoor products ordered and distributed copies. Cloud patterns were identical throughout the world, and foreign governments adopted the chart, with the captions translated into various languages.

To make his cloud photos he did not let inclement weather conditions daunt him. Once I had brought a girlfriend to Richmond from graduate school in Baltimore for the weekend, and we had gone downtown on the bus. While we were returning home late that afternoon a thunderstorm hit, and when the bus arrived at the corner of Monument and Commonwealth Avenues it was still raining steadily.

Monument Avenue was a wide thoroughfare with a grass plot running down the center, and my parents' house was located diagonally across the avenue from the bus stop, on the far corner. There was nothing for us to do when we got off the bus but to dash across the intersection through the rain.

As we sprinted toward the house I caught sight of a strange-looking black object in the center of the plot some yards away. It was no time to investigate further, but once we reached the shelter of the front door I turned around and tried to make out what it was. It was a figure, with a black shroud draped over it. The rain was slackening, and after a moment I realized it was my father. He was bent over a camera and tripod, with a black raincoat pulled over it and him, waiting to take a photograph of the sunset when the storm lifted. What my girlfriend thought about it was not reported; doubtless it confirmed certain suspicions already formed about me.

He did all the marketing of his weather booklets and charts himself, by mail. His spelling and punctuation were, to say the least, impressionistic; his approach to problems of sentence structure was to add a comma and keep going. Whether his sales methods were successful because or in spite of his epistolary technique is difficult to determine. MacLean Whittet, his publisher, once told me he thought that if the merchandising were handled professionally the sales might be considerably larger. That might well have been true; yet it is also possible that the quaintness, for want of a better term, of my father's prose style commanded attention where a more conventionally composed letter would have gone unread. What is certain, as Whittet, who was devoted to him, readily granted, is that there could be no question of its being done any other way than it was, for my father's days centered upon doing the marketing, and opening and reading the morning mail was a focal point of his existence.

Successful though the guide and chart were, predicting the forthcoming weather by cloud and wind direction was a method for short-term forecasting only. It was when my father began making long-term weather prognostications that he hit his stride. Once again, his method constituted no new scientific discovery; it was his ability to perceive the practical possibilities of a long-established phenomenon, and to persist in following its implications, that produced results.

In books about weather and climate he had read that major volcanic eruptions belched immense quantities of volcanic ash and dust into the sky overhead. These were not immediately dissipated, but instead, held in suspension in the upper atmosphere, they moved around the earth at a steady progression, traveling approximately 600 miles every twenty-four hours. The ash and dust refracted the rays of the sun, thereby altering normal weather patterns.

It followed, he reasoned, that if he could learn when and where major volcanic eruptions occurred, and measure the distance from the locations to the East Coast, he could calculate when the ash and dust would be arriving overhead, thereby producing "unusual" weather conditions in the Richmond area.

He began watching out for news of eruptions; in particular the *New York Times* regularly carried accounts of volcanic activity. For each he determined when the debris would first reach the East Coast and then, having circled the globe, appear overhead a second and a third time, with a diminished effect from each successive circumnavigation.

After several projections proved correct, he began announcing his long-range predictions, and it was not long before people started to take note. What first drew widespread attention was a prognostication, made weeks in advance, that on a specified date in early November in the mid-1950s there would be "unusual" weather. Not only that, but before it happened he advised the operator of the gasoline station he patronized to be sure to lay in a good supply of antifreeze. Ten inches of snow fell that day, weeks before it normally snowed in Richmond. The weather bureau in Richmond had given no warning. While other gasoline dealers were caught without antifreeze, my father's station did a land-office business.

Thereafter the Richmond newspapers and the local television stations were eager to have news of his predictions. He began compiling twice-yearly forecasts of future dates. Giving himself a window of twelve hours before and after each date, he predicted days of "unusual" weather up to six months in advance. He did not specify what would happen on those days. In the summer it might be no more than a drop in temperature; in the winter it could mean a blizzard.

Dispatched over the Associated Press wire to newspapers in other cities, the lists of forthcoming "Rubin Days," as they were called, became widely known throughout the state of Virginia. People clipped them out, posted them next to the telephone, and waited to see whether they arrived as predicted. Trips, outdoor weddings, and receptions were scheduled in accordance with them. Once the publisher of the Richmond newspapers, David Tennant Bryan, was in Tampa, Florida, and needed to get back to Richmond for a board meeting. Stormy weather was predicted, and the question was whether he ought to try flying home, with the risk of being stranded at an airport somewhere, or take the train, which would put him back in Richmond too late for the opening of the meeting. So he called my father, who told him, "If you can get to Atlanta, go ahead and fly. Otherwise, take the train." The Atlanta airport was still open, so Bryan traveled by airplane, and made it back in time for his meeting.

On another occasion someone had scheduled a huge outdoor wedding and reception for the afternoon before a "Rubin Day." The hostess called my father; should she make arrangements to transfer the festivities indoors?

"If you'll be through before 5 p.m.," my father told her, "go ahead with your plans." The affair came off without a hitch. A few minutes before 6 p.m. the heavens opened and a downpour drenched the city of Richmond. In gratitude, the wedding host sent my father a half-dozen bottles of imported Scotch whiskey. Neither he nor my mother drank, so he returned them.

Whenever hurricanes, snowstorms, and the like were reported to be in the offing, the newspapers called him and the television news people interviewed him and broadcast his taped comments. When a "Rubin Day" arrived as scheduled, particularly during the winter months when the result was ice and snow, headlines proclaimed that the "Weather

Wizard" had again called his shot. He was portrayed in an editorial cartoon in the *Richmond Times-Dispatch* bundled up against the winter and tossing a snowball at the bull's-eye of a target, with a little figure in the corner of the cartoon declaring, "Amazing!" He was much in demand for talks to civic and fraternal groups. With a slide projector, a carousel, and an assortment of cloud slides, he developed a program that was highly popular.

What he was in effect forecasting was the arrival of weather fronts. Within a forty-eight-hour period, which was the time claimed for a "Rubin Day" to happen, the likelihood of a front coming through was good. What seemed remarkable about his predictions, however, was the severity of the weather on the dates he cited. It was as if the normal advent of a weather front had been intensified by the arrival overhead of the dust and ash of the volcanic eruption. Nowadays meteorologists pay considerably more attention to volcanic activity as the source of weather change than was true in the 1950s and 1960s when my father was making his prognostications.

He claimed an accuracy rate of 93 per cent. When, as occasionally happened, he missed one, and "unusual" weather did not occur within twelve hours of a "Rubin Day," that too was news. His answer, when asked about it, was, "Babe Ruth struck out sometimes, too." What the professional meteorologists at the weather bureau in Richmond thought of his doings is not on record, but can be guessed. Doubtless it did not help that people were constantly making comparisons, especially after one of his Days had arrived in especially dramatic fashion. The weather bureau's forecasters, of course, could not restrict their predictions to specific dates; they were responsible for issuing forecasts every day. Moreover, when asked by interviewers, my father would reply in effect that they were doing the best they could, which no doubt comforted them mightily.

Once again, to say that such things did not go unpublicized would be a considerable understatement. Both Richmond newspapers assigned reporters to keep in touch with him. The television weathermen were regular callers. There were also features in magazines and various

BULLS-EYE!

newspapers. These did not occur accidentally; he worked at it, and was constantly sending off articles, clippings, and photographs.

On several occasions I rewrote articles for him. It was always a formidable job of translation, for his way of expressing himself on paper, as noted, was frequently less than totally lucent. He never really understood that there was anything more to writing than the automatic noting down of thoughts. In one instance he wanted me to rewrite an article on folk sayings as weather prophecies, to be accompanied by cloud photos. It took considerable doing, with not only much tele-phoning back and forth but going in search of additional adages to supplement his own. When done I typed up the article, mailed it to him, and he sold it to *Reader's Digest.* which sent him a check for $1,500.

It did not occur to him that he might have offered me part of it, nor did I expect it; writing it was assumed to be my filial duty. What did exasperate me, however, was what happened next. As the recipient of veterans' disability insurance, he was limited in the amount of money he could earn in excess of the payments, and the fee for the article placed his income well above the maximum allowed for that year. Instead of sending a check for the overage to me, which since I had written the article would certainly have been entirely legal, he returned the money to the U.S. Treasury! This at a time when, with a wife and two young children of my own and a college teacher's salary, I could have made very good use of it.

His yen for publicity was such that not even the abundant notice that went along with the Rubin Days could fully quench it. He was eager to appear on the Dave Garroway television show, and a date in July of 1956 was finally set for it. Unfortunately, the day before his scheduled appearance, the Italian ocean liner *Andrea Doria* collided with another ship and went down off Nantucket, and the appointment was called off and not subsequently rescheduled.

Anything that could become material for publicity was pressed into service. Once in the early 1960s I stopped by Richmond for a visit after an overnight trip of some kind, and while there discovered that I had failed to turn in my motel key. My father, whose curiosity was always active, tried the key in his front-door lock, and to his astonishment it worked. In the next day's newspaper appeared an item chronicling this remarkable coincidence.

He was assiduous in pursuing any reports of volcanic activity anywhere. On one occasion, while the Cold War was very much alive, he even penetrated the Iron Curtain to find out more about an eruption. Having learned that one had taken place somewhere in Siberia, he asked the Soviet embassy in Washington to secure details for him, and a few days later he received a vivid description of a powerful explosion of Mount Bezymianny on the Kamchatka Peninsula.

In his mind—apparently there was some scientific basis for it— there was a tie-in between volcanic eruptions, earthquakes, and sunspots. In the 1950s and 1960s geologists had by no means universally accepted the theory of plate tectonics, but it was generally agreed that areas of frequent volcanic activity such as the Pacific Rim were also prone to quakes. What sunspots had to do with it was and is not clear to me, but my father identified what he believed was a correlation. Presumably the presence of sunspots triggered volcanic explosions, which in turn caused shifts in the earth's crust—though perhaps it was that the shifting of the surface caused the molten rock beneath to well up; I am not sure.

Whichever it was, in the mid-1960s he proceeded to announce a date on which one or more earthquakes were likely. On the Eastern Seaboard, where there was no known volcanic activity, this did not occasion a great deal of concern. Supposedly a fault line did lead from or through Charleston to the Midwest, but it was believed to be quiescent. The Pacific Coast, however, was extremely quake-conscious, and when the newspapers in California learned of my father's predictions, they were on the telephone at once to find out more.

The result was headlines in San Diego and Los Angeles. A professional geologist was quoted as saying that predicting the dates of earthquakes was no great feat; the difficult part, he claimed, lay in identifying where the quakes were going to occur. This may have been so, but if anyone other than my father had ever forecast the specific day of an earthquake, I have never heard of it. In any event, on the announced date there was a quake, though fortunately not in an area that resulted in heavy property damage. This episode took place not long before my father's death in 1970; where the earthquake forecasting might have led had he stayed at it is unknown.

When he issued weather predictions there was often an instinctive delphic quality to them. Thus, for example, he and my mother went down to Charleston from Richmond early one fall, arriving there when a hurricane was off the coast of South Carolina and seemingly taking direct aim at the city. Asked by the afternoon newspaper whether it was likely to come ashore at Charleston, he replied that "if it doesn't come ashore within the next five hours, it won't strike Charleston." This was duly headlined "NEXT FIVE HOURS CRUCIAL, DECLARES WEATHER EXPERT," or words to that effect.

The eye of the hurricane had been identified as being fifty miles offshore from the city at the time, and was known to be moving at a steady speed of ten miles an hour, so that if it did not in fact arrive within five hours, this would almost certainly signify that the storm had altered its course. Sure enough, after five hours had elapsed the eye was still well out in the ocean, and when it did make landfall it was a hundred miles up the coast. I doubt that my father planned such wordings in advance; the element of showmanship came naturally to him.

He had long been convinced that his insomnia was so bad that he got practically no sleep at all. During the late 1940s he used to complain that his neighbor across the street was given to working noisily in his garage shop late into the night and before dawn. "That darn Meyers!" he would declare. One night about 2 A.M. he heard some noise outside and shouted down from his window, "Be quiet!" There followed the roar of an automobile speeding off. The next morning the neighbor's new DeSoto sedan, parked on the street, was discovered jacked up on wooden blocks. What my father had heard were thieves engaged in removing its tires, no more than fifty feet from his bedroom window.

By the mid-1960s his eyesight had deteriorated to a point at which he feared that he might not be able to pass the renewal test for his driver's license, so he allowed the license to lapse, while continuing to drive his car. His reflexes were not what they had been, however, and one day he failed to look both ways at an intersection and there was a minor collision. He was charged with driving an automobile with a license that had expired two years before, and given a citation to appear in court.

When his case was called up, the judge knew who he was. "Mr. Rubin," he asked, "what's the weather going to be for the next couple of days?"

My father's response was unrehearsed and immediate: "Your honor, that can depend a good deal on what happens here today!" He was let off with a promise not to drive his car any longer.

By the early 1960s my mother had begun showing signs of Parkinson's disease. During the influenza epidemic of the World War I years she had come close to dying, and apparently the incidence of Parkinson's among elderly persons who had survived the 1918–1919 epidemic was significantly high. The only remedial treatment then known was a surgical operation to sever certain nerves in the temples. Success was by no means guaranteed, but my mother insisted upon having it done. Not only did the surgery fail to relieve her condition, but thereafter she grew decidedly worse, with progressively less control of her movements, aphasia, and recessiveness. The drug L-Dopa, which was prescribed to alleviate tremor and other symptoms, had not yet been made available in the United States, but reports of it had been published, and my father was placing high hopes upon its being able to remedy my mother's situation.

Not a letter that I received from him did not begin with a lengthy description of my mother's growing infirmity and its impact upon his daily routine. Approximately every two weeks he would type out a letter with a carbon copy, one for me, one for my brother, reporting his problems. There would be several paragraphs of detailed plaint, concluding with "Cant be helped, she would have done the same if it had been me." Then would follow the news about his weather activities.

To read the extended accounts of my mother's deteriorating condition, with the same details usually repeated in letter after letter, was upsetting, the more so because there was nothing whatever that I could do about it. Probably without consciously realizing it, he wrote his letters, in part at least, to keep us reminded of what he was having to undergo; grinning and bearing it was not one of his virtues. No doubt there was no one else except my sister—who had more than enough troubles of her own at the time—to whom he could complain about such things. I came to dread seeing a letter from him in the day's mail, and would put off opening and reading it for as long as I could.

Whether for his own ailments or my mother's, my father was no Stoic. He kept detailed charts of his "nervous spells," I suppose because in his own mind their occurrence helped to corroborate and justify his inability to work. He was proud of the number and kind of medicines he took, displaying them at mealtime. "If I live for ten years I'll be lucky," he informed me once in the mid-1940s.

From as far back as I can remember I was kept well posted both on his infirmities and on his financial problems. When as a child I went off on vacation to visit relatives in Richmond or Atlanta during the summer, I was always pointedly informed that my being away would constitute his and my mother's vacation. The expense of maintaining a home and rearing a family was regularly brought to my attention. In retrospect there was a continuing and instinctive effort to instill guilt— a not-unheard-of tactic among parents.* In my own instance he succeeded very well. He could not help doing it; it was reflex action.

What is paradoxical is that his life constituted a striking refusal to yield to adversity, with a courage and resilience that overcame youthful poverty, the collapse of a hard-won business success and the abrupt loss of his health, partial paralysis, and a seemingly confined prospect for the future, to create a totally new, highly imaginative career for himself. He did *not* give in, did not acquiesce in what appeared to be devastating misfortune.

---

*And, it might be noted, a standard item of Jewish humor. As in:

A man telephones his mother in Florida. "Mom, how are you?"

"Not too good," says the mother. "I've been very weak."

The son says, "Why are you so weak?"

She says, "Because I haven't eaten in thirty-eight days."

The man says, "That's terrible. Why haven't you eaten in thirty-eight days?"

The mother answers, "Because I didn't want my mouth to be filled with food if you should remember to call."

It seems to me that the very tenacity and staunchness that made his achievement possible went along with the self-absorption that characterized his pursuit of his goals. He tended sometimes to view his children as adjuncts to his design, and to take insufficient notice of what the impact of his own preoccupations might be upon them. My brother called him once to report the mournful news that he was getting a divorce. Within thirty seconds, he said, my father was talking about his weather activities. Yet he had a strong sense of duty, and he did care deeply about our lives and careers.

In later years his life settled into a routine, built around his weather predicting. Each morning he rode the bus to the post office on Patterson Avenue. After reading his mail he walked across the avenue to wait for the return bus. By then he was so well known to so many people that more often than not a passing motorist would recognize him and give him a ride home.

Once, in 1965, I happened to be in Richmond and had driven out to the western end of the city. When done with my business I drove east along Patterson Avenue, and as I neared the post office I saw him waiting on the corner for the bus. I pulled to the curb, opened the door, and he climbed in. As I drove off he turned to me, thrust out his hand, and said, "Your face is familiar, but I forget the name!"

"Look again," I told him.

He was greatly embarrassed No doubt he thought he was losing his grip. In actuality there was nothing strange in his failure to recognize me. He was accustomed to strangers stopping at that corner to offer him a ride. I was not *supposed* to be driving eastward along Patterson Avenue in Richmond in the late morning. I was in the wrong place at the wrong time.

Before my mother was afflicted she did the cooking, and she took care to prepare and serve only dishes that he liked. Very occasionally, however, she purchased something at the grocery market that he did not care for but that she did. Once I was in town for dinner, and before the meal she told me that we were having roast duck, but not to say anything about it, because although my father did not like duck he would probably assume it was chicken.

We sat down at the accustomed time and began eating, with my father as usual paying little attention to the food itself. At length, however, he said to my mother, "I'd like some white meat."

"This chicken doesn't have any white meat," she told him.

My father continued eating. He was, however, thinking over what she had said. "I never heard of a chicken that doesn't have white meat," he declared after an interval.

"This one doesn't," my mother said.

He considered that for a minute. Then he had an idea. "This isn't a duck, is it?"

"Now, don't worry about it," my mother said. "Just eat your dinner."

Whatever he may have suspected, he made no further comment.

He wanted to write a book about the weather, but since writing was not among his skills, he would need a collaborator. At one point a newspaper reporter tried to work with him on it, but without success. What was required was someone who was experienced in writing about scientific subjects for general readers. I happened to know one such in Roanoke, and put him in touch with my father.

It turned out to be an ideal pairing. My father had the interpreter he needed. The result was a book-length manuscript which was sold to a book packager in New York City and placed with a publishing firm, Franklin Watts. Set in large type for use in school science courses, the book went into page proof, to be published in the fall of 1970. My father had a set spiral-bound and was eagerly anticipating marketing and promoting it in his own inimitable fashion. He told a friend of mine that he was going to outsell any of my books—which would constitute even less of a feat than he probably realized.

On July 30, 1970, he suffered a massive cerebral hemorrhage, and died late that morning. He was seventy-five years old.

It was front-page news in Richmond. The television stations all aired brief documentaries. He had already arranged for cremation, and a local television weatherman who was an airplane pilot had agreed to take his ashes aloft and strew them over the city. "When there's a thunderstorm," my father had said, "they'll say, 'Old Man Rubin's at it again!'" He had even made arrangements for the television stations to photograph the airplane as it took off, though when my Aunt Dora learned of this, she insisted that the cameras be kept away.

Flowers, telegrams, and letters poured in. At the funeral service the mortuary chapel was packed. In the pocket of my father's suit, partly visible as his body lay in the coffin, the mortician had placed a copy of his weather booklet.

My mother could not attend; by then her decline was too pronounced. She died in 1982.

Forecasting the Weather, by Louis D. Rubin, Sr., with the Assistance of Hiram J. Herbert, was published in September of 1970 in an edition of ten thousand copies. Without the author available to promote it, the book sold out its printing in a couple of years, and was not reissued.

In the early 1980s I started a publishing company, Algonquin Books, and one of our first projects was to bring out my father's book in a new edition. More than a decade had gone by since its publication, and not only my father but Hiram J. Herbert were dead. The basic premises of the book, to portray cloud sequences and explain how to use them to predict developments in the weather, remained sound, but it would be necessary for the text to take account of more recent developments in weather science. A meteorologist for one of the Richmond television stations was secured to rework the text as appropriate.

With a new introduction telling about my father and his projects, *The Weather Wizard's Cloud Book,* by Louis D. Rubin, Sr., and Jim Duncan with the Assistance of Hiram H. Herbert, subtitled *How You Can Forecast the Weather Accurately and Easily by Reading the Clouds,* was published by Algonquin Books in the fall of 1984 in a paperback edition. There were more than 120 cloud photographs in full color. Over the years the book has sold steadily, with regular reprintings as needed. In 1991, after I had retired, Algonquin published *The Weather Wizard's Five-Year Weather Diary*, in spiral binding. Algonquin's senior editor, the Weather Wizard's grandson, my son Robert Alden Rubin, compiled the book, which is also a steady seller.

My father has been dead, as I write this, for many years now. Yet there are people, in Richmond and elsewhere in Virginia, who when they hear my name at once ask whether I am any relation to the man who used to predict Rubin Days. He was my father, I tell them, and they are impressed, for he is remembered fondly. To echo Samuel Johnson on the actor David Garrick, it might be said that his death "eclipsed the gaiety of nations, and impoverished the publick stock of harmless pleasure"—in both instances an exaggeration, to be sure, but as Johnson also remarked, when composing a lapidary inscription a man is not upon oath.

He was one of a kind. During all the years since his death I don't suppose a day has gone by when I have not thought of him. In particular when there is a notable natural phenomenon—the eruption of Mount St. Helens in 1980, Hurricane Hugo which devastated Charleston and the Southeast in 1989, the San Francisco Bay area earthquake which disrupted the World Series that year, a record snowfall, a blizzard—my first thought is inevitably, "If only the Weatherman could be here for this." My brother and I joke about him sometimes. If one of us is held up by a severe storm and his plane arrives at its destination several hours late, the other will say, "He sure fixed your wagon this time, didn't he?" He remains a presence in our lives. Take him all in all, there was no else remotely like him.

7

Vocations

MY FATHER WAS THE FIFTH child and youngest son. A sister, Esther, was born in 1897, and another, Ruth, in 1902. When Hyman Levy Rubin was disabled by a heart attack that year, the two youngest children, Esther and Ruthie, were kept in Charleston rather than being sent away to the Hebrew Orphans' Home in Atlanta. Later, when family finances eased, they were the only two of the children to attend high school.

Esther, or Essie as she was always called, became the housekeeper in the early 1910s. A soft-voiced, gentle person, she was the only one of the sisters to marry. Her husband, Sol Gadalia Cohen, was a clothing salesman. They lived in Columbia, South Carolina, during the late 1930s and the 1940s, but Essie made lengthy stays in Charleston with her oldest sister, Dora. With the naïveté of the young, it never occurred to me to wonder why. Not until the late 1940s, when Sol was sent to prison and Essie came to stay with our family in Richmond, did I become aware that Sol was a compulsive gambler and throughout their marriage was recurrently in trouble. In Richmond, having no source of income, Essie went looking for employment for the first time in her life. After Sol was discharged in 1950, she was preparing to return to him, when he died. Thereafter, until her own death in 1989, Essie lived in Charleston, working for some years for the Chamber of Commerce. She was kind, even-tempered, affectionate; her life was spent caring for people—her brothers and sisters, then her husband, and in later years her sisters. I never once heard her complain about her lot.

Ruthie, called that to distinguish her from her sister-in-law Ruth, my Uncle Harry's wife, was very different in disposition. At the time that the family was going through its ordeal she was an infant. As an adult she worked as a stenographer and secretary in Charleston, Jacksonville, and, from the mid-1930s until she retired in the late 1960s, in Columbia. After that she returned to Charleston. Strong-willed, independent, set in her ways, she made few friends of her own. Her interests and concerns were highly personal; except for some volunteer work for the American Cancer Society she participated in no group activities. She was eighty-six when Essie died, and my sister Joan moved down from Richmond to live with her. Ruthie's rigidity made her difficult to look after. For the last several years she had nurses around the clock, and she did not Go Gentle into That Good Night. When she died in 2000, the last of her generation, she was ninety-eight.

My Rubin grandparents, my aunts and uncles, and my mother are buried in the family plot at the K. K. Beth Elohim cemetery on Huguenin Avenue—all the brothers and sisters except for my father, whose ashes were scattered in the sky above Richmond. My sister has arranged to be buried there, and I should like to be, in order to be with my father's people—though there may not be room for me. When the time comes, however, I do not expect that it will concern me a great deal one way or the other.

If there is any existence after death, it will surely not involve corporeal resurrection. I remember something my father said. We were at a funeral in Richmond, and he had wandered away from the group at the graveside to look around. Presently he returned. "Come with me, there's something I want to show you," he told me. I followed him over to a nearby plot.

"I've finally found an honest man," he declared and, with the kind of macabre humor characteristic of the family, pointed to a single small stone bearing only the initials "P. U." Mark Twain, who likewise found humor in the odor of corruption, would have appreciated the observation.

When I visit Charleston nowadays I usually go out to the cemetery and look around, not only at my own family's plot but the others there as well. It is certainly an exercise in the meaning of aging, for I can remember the majority of those whose names are visible on the gravestones. More than that, I can recall something of the social distinctions and gradations that were involved, for my mother was highly conscious of such things and my sister and I had been schooled in them. This was less true of my brother, who was the youngest and the least exposed to such tutelage. How absurd it all seems now. Time, the lessons of the Holocaust, the process of Americanization have irretrievably altered what once seemed formidable divisions.

I think of the K. K. Beth Elohim Sabbath School in the 1930s. There were only two other members of my class. The entire student body, from tots to mid-teenagers, when convened in the tabernacle, could not have comprised as many as thirty children, and probably fewer than that. Had it not been for an influx of new residents during and after World War II, and the switch to Reform Judaism of many who earlier had belonged to the local Orthodox synagogues, it seems likely that the congregation of K. K. Beth Elohim would by now have withered away into extinction.

During my last several years of Sabbath School, until confirmed at sixteen, I was required to attend Saturday morning services in the temple next door, where the only other boy my age, Jack Pinkussohn, and I alternated at going up to the altar at a designated point during the service and helping Rabbi Raisin remove the Torah from the ark and unroll it on the altar, so that he could read from it.

It was my task to place the elaborate silver ornaments and breastplate on a chair, help him ease off the embroidered velvet jacket, then after he completed the reading, replace the ornaments and hold the sacred scroll upright on my lap while he read the day's passage from the large bound volume containing the whole of the Old Testament. The Torah would then be returned to the ark, and I could go back down to our family pew.

Although I had not yet begun reading books of archaeology and anthropology, what used to occur to me even then was that it was almost as if I were cradling the body of a child, which I had helped to undress and to dress, and that the shape of the scroll vaguely corresponded with arms, legs, and torso. "And they came to the place which God told him of, and Abraham built an altar there, and laid the wood in order, and bound Isaac his son, and laid him on the altar upon the wood." What is fascinating about Jewish ritual is the way in which its roots go so far into prehistory, all the way back, indeed, to a Semitic volcano-god. (My father would have liked that.)

Of the four brothers, my father was the only one who as an adult remained an active member of the congregation. There was a period in the 1930s, after his illness, when the family said prayers before supper on Friday night, and he even purchased a seven-branched candelabrum and some religious books. (I doubt that he read very far into any of the books.) He was also a member of the K.K.B.E. Temple Brotherhood, attending its monthly meetings. I am reminded of his account of one such meeting, in which he got up and made a comment on what was being discussed, following which a family friend, Joe Fatman, rose to express approval of his remarks. "Mr. Rubin," Joe declared, "has hit the nail right on the point!"

After he moved to Richmond my father occasionally attended Friday night services, though I do not recall his doing so during his later years, and certainly not after my mother began to show symptoms of Parkinson's disease. I do not think that Judaism *as a theology*—the qualification is important—was an important element in his life.

It is scarcely a coincidence that the three older brothers, Harry, Dan, and Manning, were the family's intellectuals, so to speak, the only ones who were habitual readers, and were also the conscious nonbelievers. They were not atheists, so much as skeptics and agnostics; they could not believe in a revealed divinity, view the Holy Scriptures as His Word, or think of the Jews as the Chosen People. Of the sisters, all three were temple-goers.

In all this, and in what follows, a distinction must be made between Judaism as a religious faith, whether Reform or otherwise, and Judaism as an ethnic and social identity—and as a way of looking at the world. In point of fact the basic theological requirements of Judaism may be seen as minimal: "It hath been told thee, O man, what is good, and what the Lord requireth of thee: to do justly, to love mercy, and to walk humbly with thy God." Obviously one does not cease to be a Jew because one disbelieves in Mosaic law or cannot credit the direct intervention of a divinity who adheres to a policy of visiting the iniquities of the fathers upon the children unto the third and fourth generation of them that hate Him.

So far as I know, none of my father's family ever desired either to deny or to disguise the fact of his or her Jewish identity. I cannot imagine any of them ever doing so. Depending on the circumstances under which one lived and worked, however, being a Jew could have different manifestations and involve varying degrees of self-consciousness. During the summer of my sophomore year in college I worked for a weekly newspaper in North Charleston. The editor and owner was Jewish, and on one occasion I asked him why, since I was supposedly the sports editor, my name was not so listed on the masthead. "Too much Palestinian ancestry," he told me. I was shocked; it had never occurred to me that there was reason to conceal that identity, and I much resented the assumption.

I once stayed with a black friend in Louisiana, and that evening, in company with his wife and a neighbor who had played professional football, we watched a National Football League game on television. As the game went on, the three of them discussed the players on the field, and what impressed me was how important it was to them to identify which players were and were not black. "He's black," they would at once say when a particular player was highlighted on the screen. Or, "He's white." Obviously, and understandably, when the milieu which they were watching was one involving both blacks and whites, race was a key fact of identity and extremely important to them. I think they had forgotten I was present. When at one point my friend's wife abruptly remembered that I was there, she laughed apologetically. "Oh, Louis doesn't mind us," she said.

The incident made me realize the extent to which, even among highly educated black professionals, the experience of racial discrimination had permeated every facet of their lives. It also made me understand something of what it must have been like to be an immigrant Jew, speaking English only imperfectly and with a European accent, in late-nineteenth-century America.

When my father and his brothers and sisters were children, being Jewish must surely have been set them apart from their neighbors. (So, also, must having been very poor.) Once they became adults, however, to a considerable degree this ceased to be true. There is a photograph of my father, taken in the 1920s, seated with a group of the city's electrical contractors and retail merchants. He is both the youngest member and, I believe, the only Jew in the photo. One would assume that he must initially have been quite conscious of being both. Yet it is also likely that once he believed himself a fully accepted part of the group, and that his relationships with the other electrical merchants were not importantly conditioned by either his racial identity or his age, he would thereafter have used other criteria than those to define his ties both with the individuals in the group and with the group itself.

It is not that he would think of himself as other than a Jew or would attempt to suppress that aspect of his identity. But that he was Jewish, and that his fellow electrical merchants were or were not Jewish, would have ceased in his mind to be a major defining factor in his relations with them.

This, I believe, is one reason why Jews who have grown up in large Jewish communities, where many, if not the majority, of their associates are also Jewish, often find it difficult to understand other Jews, and in particular those in Reform Jewish families, who grow up and live in small Southern cities and towns. Once the process of assimilation begins to take effect, it can move with considerable swiftness, with the result that whether someone is or is not Jewish, or whether someone else is, will cease to be an immediate item of definition. I do not think that it is possible to understand my father, his brothers, or his sisters without keeping in mind that certainly for their adult lives, as well as for much of their childhood, by far the larger part of their acquaintance, whether professional or social, was with non-Jews, so that in their everyday existence they were not likely to assume that their Jewish identity, as such, set them crucially apart from their neighbors.

At the same time, that very fact helps to explain why, in the instances of Reform Jews such as my Uncle Harry, my Aunt Ruthie, and my own mother, there was some feeling of looking down on less assimilated Jews, whose presence was a reminder of their own origins and their differences from their everyday associates. Not surprisingly, as the process of Americanization has continued apace, and the large body of Russian and eastern European Jews who thronged into the United States in the early twentieth century have become assimilated, the occasion for that particular form of snobbery has receded. The catastrophe of the World War II years also served to demonstrate the emptiness of such supposed distinctions.

The relentless process of Americanization is one of the reasons there has been a movement within the present Reform Jewish community toward a return to some of the traditional Jewish rituals which were discarded in the nineteenth century. The ceremonial rite of Bar Mitzvah, for example, in which upon reaching puberty the Jewish boy demonstrates from the altar of the synagogue his ability to read and to chant passages of Hebrew and is thereby admitted into the congregation, has been revived. Until recent years Reform Jewish youths were not Bar Mitzvah; they were confirmed—not at the age of twelve or thirteen but fifteen or sixteen—and did not study Hebrew or learn to read aloud in it. At the same time this custom—which is not biblical but fifteenth-century in origin—has been expanded to include girls, or Bas Mitzvah, an innovation quite without traditional sanction.

The institution of the rabbi singing, or canting, the Jewish prayer service rather than reading it, which had been entirely discarded in Reform ritual, is also being revived—rather to the dislike of some of the older congregation members. The return to traditional ritual is selective, to be sure. Males and females are not segregated into separate areas of the synagogue; skullcaps known as yarmulkes are not required headgear for males when worshiping; choirs and hymn-singing, which were Reform Jewish innovations, have not been dropped, nor has the playing of organ music; circumcision is not a religious rite, to be performed by a rabbi; and so on.

In company with the liberalizing theological motivations that in the nineteenth century had prompted the development of Reform Judaism, there was also the wish to conduct worship in a form more nearly resembling that in the Protestant churches. This involved, among other things, the elimination of much of the ceremony that had been conducted in Hebrew, the more so because very few members of the congregation could read or speak it. Religions thrive on ritual, however, and since by the mid–twentieth century the position of Jews in American life had become considerably less separate and isolated, the concern now took the opposite form—a fear that with the decline of traditional ritual went the fading of Jewish identity, and that the practice of Judaism itself was in need of reinforcement.

This phenomenon, which closely corresponds to a similar movement in the Roman Catholic Church, is thus not a manifestation of a feeling of separation from the secular community. On the contrary, it is possible only because, as the process of cultural and social assimilation has continued, the assertion of a separate Jewish religious identity no longer poses a threat to individual status within that community. Reform Jewish children were once named Henry, Arthur, Edgar; their children are named Jacob, David, and Simon. The same dynamics are at work which once led Americans of Irish ancestry to christen their children John, Richard, and James, and that now cause them to be named Kevin, Patrick, and Sean.

In my own father's family, as already noted, of the four sons only my father continued his Reform Jewish affiliation as an adult. I do not know for sure what the religious views—as distinct from the social and political views—of the oldest son, my Uncle Harry, were, but I doubt very much that he was a believer. Obviously my two other uncles, Dan and Manning, were not.

What their father, my grandfather, thought about the observance of Jewish custom is unknown. A prayer book, in English and Hebrew, exists in which he recorded the names of his children with their Jewish equivalents. That his oldest child, my Aunt Dora, who was in her early twenties when he died in 1911, was the one who adhered most closely to Jewish religious customs might indicate that she was following her father's lead. But that is only a surmise, and of course it may be significant that he appears to have maintained no contact by mail with his family back in East Prussia, where his father was either a rabbi or a religious teacher. Certainly my Aunt Dora was told nothing whatever about them by him. However, not too much can be made of that, for there is no way of knowing whether either of his parents was still alive by the time he came to Charleston in the 1880s and married.

Nor was it uncommon for immigrant parents to say little or nothing to their children about their childhood in central and eastern Europe. They wished to put that life behind them, and their children to grow up with as little encumbrance as possible to their identity as American citizens. My mother's father in Richmond, for example, who was born in Austria and emigrated as a young man, would not allow Yiddish to be spoken in his home; he made a sharp distinction between religious observance and the culture of the only recently vacated central European ghetto. My assumption is that the same was true of my father's parents, for not once did I ever hear any of their children use a Yiddish expression. (The result was that I grew up so totally ignorant of "the joys of Yiddish" that when in the early 1940s I listened to "Allen's Alley" on the radio and Mrs. Nussbaum answered the door with "Nu?" I thought the humor consisted of her saying "No?" instead of "Yes?")

In my family's instance there was obviously, during the 1910s and 1920s, a conscious intent to adopt the mores of the secular community. Thus both my first cousin and I were named after our fathers, with "Junior" appended, which in Ashkenazi—not Sephardic—Jewish custom was never done. In my instance the nomenclature is somewhat confusing, in that my father was named after the physician who delivered him, Louis Decimus Barbot. In lineage I was ranked therefore as both second and tenth. I suppose I should be grateful that the physician was not named Decimus Brutus.

I think my mother would have liked the practice to be continued with my firstborn son, with "III" appended, but having endured being called "Junior" throughout my boyhood I had no intention of fastening any such designation on a child of mine. (It was the rule, in the racially segregated South of those days, for black domestics to use "Mister" once the male children of the house became teenagers, so when I turned thirteen our family cook was expected to address me as "Mr. Junior." After I received my Ph.D. our friend Hasell Rivers proposed that henceforth I be called "Dr. Junior.")

More or less the same process was at work for all but a few of the Reform Jewish families in Charleston. There were other "Juniors." I can recall only a single young male who had grown up in the congregation being Bar Mitzvah, and he was the rabbi's son. Our family observed the High Holy Days and the various festivals, and my parents attended temple services on Friday night. Beyond that, however, their lives did not center on Jewish social activities; indeed, other than my mother's weekly sewing circle there were no such activities. As for myself, I had no close Jewish friends; there were none who lived anywhere near me, at school none who shared my intellectual and journalistic interests, and only one Jewish boy who played sandlot baseball, in which from March through September I was passionately engaged. To be both a Reform Jew and a teenager in Charleston in the 1930s was hardly a communal activity.

When I think of my father and his three brothers in relationship to their own father, what seems striking is the contrast with his passivity. Granted that Hyman Rubin could write English only very haltingly, that apparently he was not robust and from the early 1900s onward suf-

fered from a disabling heart condition, even so there seems to be a
sense almost of apathy about him. My Aunt Dora, as noted earlier, said
that as a merchant he was too trusting. Even the comment that the
judge in Florence made after his death, quoting St. Paul to describe him
as "an Israelite in whom there was no guile," has as its corollary that he
was guileless—which is to say, innocent, naïve.

This is not to say that his sons, by contrast, were guileful. If there
was any wiliness about any of them, certainly it does not show up in
their careers. Of the two who were in business, my father, until his illness, was the more successful, but he too proved to be overly trustful,
placing too great a continued reliance upon the employee who was left
in charge while he was incapacitated. Subsequently there was a naïveté
about his weather-predicting activities that if anything enhanced their
attractiveness, but it also manifested itself in financial arrangements
that, once the demand for his booklet and chart was established, could
have been more profitably renegotiated. (It has been said that the venture of his elder son in forming a publishing house, Algonquin Books,
was marked by a similar naïveté, resulting in an editorial but decidedly
not a financial success.)

Still, apparently unlike their father's, the lives of the four brothers
can in no way be said to have been characterized by passivity or
lethargy. I think of the three younger boys returning from the Orphans'
Home to make their way on their own. Through hard work, one became a Broadway playwright, another a newspaper columnist and editor. As for my father, whose forte was not writing and reading, surely
to teach himself electricity and manage two separate, successive careers
was anything but acquiescence in a disadvantaged situation. Even the
oldest brother, Harry, though not a conspicuously successful businessman, earned a reasonably good living for his family and achieved the
particular form of respect that he coveted. When one considers where
they started from, what they did can only be called remarkable. Clearly
they did not lack ambition, nor the energy and determination to act
upon that ambition.

Yet despite their early poverty and disadvantages, and what must have been the considerable humiliation involved, it is noteworthy that in none of them does the acquisitive instinct appear to have been foremost or even very important in their subsequent lives. I do not mean that they disdained financial gain, but rather that it would be difficult to interpret their choice of vocations and the conduct of their lives as having been shaped by it.

Dan, for example, deliberately relinquished a lucrative assignment as a writer of movie scripts, at which he was clearly very good, in order to return to writing plays. Certainly he hoped that his future works would enjoy the commercial success of his previous two Broadway plays, yet realistically he must have known that year in and year out he could hardly expect his earnings from writing for the stage to come close to what Paramount Studios was paying him. Nor is there the slightest indication that, after several years of not having his new plays produced, he made any move to return to film writing. He had earned enough money to do the kind of writing he wanted; that was what mattered to him.

His brother Manning, having become his newspaper's top reporter and then its city editor and columnist, could surely have moved on to papers of greater circulation and larger salaries. Instead he stayed in Charleston; neither money nor journalistic renown could lure him elsewhere. As for my father, it was the show, the sheer, splendid exhibition, that always prompted him, whether as businessman, rose gardener, or forecaster of "unusual weather."

The three younger brothers were endowed with powerful creative streaks. What was their origin? To be sure, the tracing of hereditary characteristics is a chancy business. The notion that so-and-so "takes after" this or that forebear or forebears can be carried to ridiculous conclusions. Yet there does seem to be a persistent pattern, or aptitude, in the behavior of the family—although, if so, the women would appear to have been denied the necessary basic opportunity and encouragement for it to develop. Seemingly it was absent in the makeup of their father. Where, then, did it come from?

The obvious place to look is across the ocean. What little is known of Hyman Rubin's father, Herschel, is to the effect that he was either a religious teacher or rabbi and that he came from a "fine family," which, as noted earlier, in the context of the eastern European ghetto would almost certainly have meant not wealth or secular eminence, but the only kind of distinction that could be effectively passed down among the Jews within the Pale of Settlement, as it was known throughout the bounds of the Tsarist Russian empire: that is, recognition as a rabbi and custodian of Jewish law and custom. In Isaiah Berlin's description of inhabitants of the Jewish enclaves, "their lives were bound up with religious observance, and their minds and hearts were filled with the images and symbolism of Jewish history and religion to a degree scarcely intelligible in western Europe since the waning of the Middle Ages" ("Chaim Weizman," *Personal Impressions,* ed. Henry Hardy).

By the mid– to late nineteenth century this insular, self-contained community life had begun to break up; Hyman Rubin's emigration and arrival in the New World was a manifestation of its crumbling. It is significant that my Aunt Dora, when asked about him, told me that "he should have been a scholar," which evidently was the family tradition. If so, then as a young man without funds, without any kind of special vocational knowledge, living in a country whose language he knew only very imperfectly, he was singularly ill-equipped to follow along in the tradition. As a child and youth he must have been schooled in his father Herschel's religious training, but there is no indication that he was notably interested in Judaism, even while a career as a secular scholar in America would have been out of the question for him.

When he and his wife first came down to Charleston to join her sister Rose and her family, he worked as a clerk in a wholesale grocery firm. As the children began arriving, he moved to increase what could only have been a very modest income by operating little shops of his own in a succession of Lowcountry South Carolina towns. The result was anything but remunerative, and when in 1902 he became unable to work there was acute financial distress.

Once his sons, victims of that distress, reached an age at which they could act to extricate themselves, they went to work doing just that. Not only did they possess, in different ways and to varying degrees, the vitality that their father seemingly lacked, but they were not handicapped by a language barrier that set them apart from other Americans, nor were they steeped in what for them in their secular situation would have seemed a body of largely useless knowledge and lore. As American youths they were in effect freed from the limits and barriers of the ghetto, both geographically and imaginatively, and there would seem to have been almost an explosion of intellectual energy—as if the traditional aptitudes of their European forebears were now liberated and could be applied to the needs and the opportunities of secular American experience. "Only in America . . . "

Not to the pursuit of wealth as such, however, but of the kind of achievement that, in the closed milieu that their father had set behind him when he left for the New World, had taken the form of religious schooling and rabbinical dedication. It was intellectual and creative vocation that they sought.

The best word to characterize the conduct of their lives, all in all, might well be "religious"—though not in the sense of believing in a revealed, codified, and dogmatized God, whether that of Reform Judaism or any other, since clearly they did not so believe. Rather, religious as in "scrupulously faithful or exact; strict; conscientious; zealous; fervent; devout; as, to follow one's advice with *religious* care" (*Webster's New International Dictionary of the English Language*, 2d ed.) This was their paternal heritage, and, transplanted into a secular society, it appears to have manifested itself in a different, but no less conscientious and fervent, way than it must have done for their grandfather Herschel and their rabbinical forebears in the ghettos of eastern Europe.

In the lives of the three younger boys, who were the ones I knew best, the inheritance seems unmistakable. I think of my Uncle Dan in his later years, faithfully writing play after play, two a year, for two decades and more, without ever having another accepted for production. Of my Uncle Manning, seated out on the rocks at the foot of Beaufain Street by the river, reading; he loved learning, for its own sake.

I think of my father. Surely the explanation for that hooded figure out on the grass plot on Monument Avenue, waiting with his camera in pouring-down rain to photograph the sunset, may be accurately expressed as "dedicated."

They could be obsessive, self-absorbed, compulsive; their political and social views could be narrow-minded, even bigoted. They could be too trusting, naïve. But I never knew one of them to be selfish, stingy, tricky, or dishonest; to seek to take advantage of anyone else's misfortune, innocence, or credulity; to cheat or knowingly to mislead anyone. They were never duplicitous. They maintained a lofty, absolute ethical standard. Nothing less was conceivable to any of them.

Those years in the Orphans' Home were decidedly the generative force in their youthful lives. It marked them, powerfully, profoundly. Whatever they did thereafter was in response to having been sent away to live in an institution, among strangers in a strange city. I have copies of the applications that their mother filed to secure admission for the three boys into the orphanage, which was founded in 1876 to provide help for the children of needy eastern European immigrants, of whom there were many. To read them, even across the span of a hundred years, is rending.

Each application, dated August 12, 1902, and apparently filled out by the boys' aunt, Rose Hoffman, began with the child's name and place and date of birth: "Daniel Rubin, Charleston, S.C. Aug. 4, 1892"; "Manning Rubin, Charleston, S.C. December 11, 1894 [1893]"; "Louis Rubin Charleston, S.C. May 31, 1895."

"*Nationality of father:* Russian.

"*Nationality of mother:* American.

"*Is either father or mother living?* Both, but Father is an invalid and Mother alone with 7 children depending upon the public for support.

"*What means of support has the child?* None whatever."

There are questions about health, and "*Has the child any vicious habits?* No, very well-behaved" for Dan and Manning, "No, very quiet child"(!) for my father,

"*How much will the family of the child contribute toward the child's maintenance?* Nothing."

At the close of each application are the child's signature and address. Dan's are in his own handwriting; he was ten years old. Manning's first name is in his handwriting, the rest in his aunt's; he was eight. My father was seven; his name and address have been filled in for him.

How frightened those three little boys must have been, uprooted from their homes. And how helpless must their family have felt, and ashamed: "depending upon the public for support." I know that all his life my father remained grateful for the care that was taken of them.

Such opportunities as they had once they returned home—and these were very few—they made the most of, to the best of their considerable ability. Still, they had advantages, too. They were Americans, and they were Jews. These were enough.